A JAPANESE TOUCH
FOR YOUR GARDEN

YOUR GARDEN

KODANSHA INTERNATIONAL LTD. Tokyo, New York, San Francisco

CREDITS AND ACKNOWLEDGMENTS: This book is based on *Sakutei no Jiten* (Encyclopedia of garden making), published in Japanese by Kodansha, Tokyo (1978). The English text was adapted and edited by Peter Goodman. The Kawabata quote on page 23 is from *Beauty and Sadness*, translated by Howard Hibbett (New York: Alfred A. Knopf, 1975, p. 91). The Okakura quote on page 6 is from *The Book of Tea*, with a foreword and biographical sketch by Elise Grilli (Reprint. Rutland, Vt. and Tokyo: Charles E. Tuttle, 1956, p. 62). The Sadler quote on page 7 is from *Cha-no-yu: The Japanese Tea Ceremony* (Reprint. Rutland, Vt. and Tokyo: Charles E. Tuttle: 1962, p. 29). The Tange quote on page 7 is from *Ise: Prototype of Japanese Architecture* (Cambridge, Mass.: MIT Press, 1965, p. 22).

The editor would like to thank the following for their assistance: Tsutomu Abe, Takashi Akimoto, Tadashi Kanai, Noda Zōen Co., Ltd., Akira Ōhira, Yasuo Sasaki, Takuma Tono, and Atsunosuke Umesawa.

Line drawings were prepared by Design System Inc., Yoshito Suzuki, and Zenjirō Tagomori. All color photos are by Haruzō Ōhashi except: 124–31, by Tadashige Ōhashi.

LOCATIONS OF GARDENS SHOWN IN THE PHOTOS (private gardens are not listed; "K" stands for "Kyoto")—*22:* Joei-ji, Yamaguchi. *23:* Shinnyo-in, K. *24:* Rakuraku-en, Shiga. *26:* Ryoan-ji, K. *27, 29:* Daitoku-ji, K. *31:* Ryugen-in, K. *35:* Saiho-ji, K. *38:* Erin-ji, K. *39:* Tenryu-ji, K. *50:* Katsura Rikyu, K. *51:* Ryugen-in, K. *52:* Daisen-in, K. *53:* Kogaku-ji, Yamanashi. *56, 57:* Tenryu-ji, K. *58:* Sainan-in, Wakayama. *59:* Daisen-in, K. *61–63:* Katsura Rikyu, K. *64:* Konji-in, K. *65:* Katsura Rikyu, K. *88:* Fujita Art Museum, Osaka. *91:* Shukukei-en, Hiroshima. *93:* Keirin-ji, Yamanashi. *94:* Warabi no Sato, K. *95:* Sanjusangen-do, K. *96:* Katsura Rikyu, K. *97:* Sento Gosho, K. *98:* Toko-en, Tottori. *100:* Ritsurin Koen, Kagawa. *101:* Koraku-en, Okayama. *102:* Toko-en, Tottori.

Distributed in the United States by Kodansha International/USA Ltd. through Harper & Row, Publishers, Inc., 10 East 53rd Street, New York, New York 10022.

Published by Kodansha International Ltd., 12–21, Otowa 2-chome, Bunkyo-ku, Tokyo 112 and Kodansha International/USA Ltd., 10 East 53rd Street, New York, New York 10022 and 44 Montgomery Street, San Francisco, California 94104.

First edition, 1980
Third printing, 1981

LCC 79–66238
ISBN 0–87011–391–7
JBC 2076–787501–2361

CONTENTS

INTRODUCTION

"[In the garden] he wished to create the attitude of a newly-awakened soul still lingering amid shadowy dreams of the past, yet bathing in the sweet unconsciousness of a mellow spiritual light, and yearning for the freedom that lay in the expanse beyond."

—Okakura Kakuzo

It is morning. The man has washed and put on a blue suit. He is now sitting quietly while he sips a cup of tea and stares off into the landscape before him. A large rugged mountain rises in the west; it is not so far away that he can't hear the splash of the waterfall it conceals. A stream rushes to the plain and feeds a lake that widens almost to his feet. The man traces the shoreline to a dense forest on the other side; the trees in front are twisted, and he can almost hear the wind that has played upon them over the years. Behind, tall cedars rise up a hill to a secluded mountain temple.

There are distances beyond that forest he would like to travel someday. But now there is no time. The man picks up his briefcase, tells his wife he will be back late that evening, and, once outside the gate, steps vigorously into the line of people already hurrying to the train station, about a five-minute walk away. . . .

The landscape the man was looking at was not a real landscape at all, but a Japanese garden only a few meters square. He built it himself. The "mountain" was a large stone he had brought in by truck. The "waterfall" and the "stream" were smaller stones and pebbles carefully arranged in clefts and tiers. The "sea" was of white gravel, and the "windswept trees" were a few pines he trained when they were young. The "hill" was made with soil removed during contouring, and the "secluded temple" was suggested by a stone tower purchased at a local garden-supply store.

But not once while looking at this scene, though he looks at it every morning, did the man say to himself, "This is just a garden." What he saw was a *landscape*: alive, unsullied, vast, and serene. It prepared him for his day in the city that lay beyond the garden wall.

Most Western-style gardens are admired for their formal beauty; their careful geometries celebrate the rational precision of their makers. They also offer colorful flowers or food for the table. The Japanese garden is no less contrived than its Western counterpart. But its rhythms and patterns—reproducing and symbolizing those of the landscape in the world outside—are established in such a way as to disguise the human hand behind them. Garden stones and trees are laid out asymmetrically to suggest the rugged wildness of nature. Permanent greens, grays, and browns predominate, but they are counterpointed by scattered flowers and fruits that mark time's passage with cycles of change. Empty space, wind, periods of dormancy, shadows, and viewing angles are subtler but full-function design elements that deepen the garden's relationship to its site. Abstract renderings of moving water in solid stone and gravel provoke the mind with their union of seeming opposites. Such dense interplays produce the effect of seeing nature whole, even though the garden may take up no more than a corner of a yard and consist only of bamboo, a shrub, and a stone.

"Driven by the compulsion to make the invisible, mysterious forces of nature and space tangible, man saw one particular substance stand out in the gloom of primeval nature—solid, immovable rock."
—Kenzo Tange

The Japanese are certainly not the only people who love nature. But there is probably no society where nature as a theme—as a measure of "quality"—has been more effectively used to shape all manner of human expression, everything from architecture, aikido, and poetry to the flowers that bus drivers keep on their dashboards. Gardening is among the older examples: manmade "micromountains" and "microlakes" have been found that date as far back as the 7th century A.D. These early gardens were based on those of T'ang China, but they came more and more to resemble the landscape of Japan itself—an island country, mountainous, full of streams and stands of tall trees. Buddhist themes were explored, but likely at the heart of the gardens—and this is just as true today—was the ancient Japanese faith of Shinto, which viewed the world and everything in it, including man, as infused with the primeval forces of creation.

From the 8th to 11th centuries, the aristocracy in Japan built large pond gardens as places for amusement. Here were complete compositions that represented smaller versions of vast expanses with islands, waterfalls, and naturalistic plantings of trees. Often, features of the distant scenery beyond were incorporated—"borrowed"—into the garden designs to increase their grandeur.

From about the middle of the 13th century, the scale of gardens was reduced. In the 15th and 16th centuries, water features like seas and waterfalls came to be represented by gravel and stone alone. This abstract strain was derived from the spirit of Zen Buddhism, which stressed simplicity and valued the provocative. Tea gardens also developed about this time. They had the practical function of creating the right mood of austerity for the tea ceremony conducted nearby. But the techniques used in them to create a natural appearance and an atmosphere of quiet taste and elegant simplicity typified the period and have had an enormous impact on garden making and Japanese aesthetics and design ever since.

"[The garden] should be naturally clean like a forest glade, but not aggressively neat. Therefore the Tea Masters considered that a boy or an old man . . . was best entrusted with the [sweeping and cleaning], because they would not be too painstaking. Leaves that have been blown about under the trees and between the stones look interesting and should not be disturbed."
—A. L. Sadler

This book introduces you to the materials used in the Japanese garden. It is designed to get you into the garden, planning and building. Explanations are arranged by theme and are mechanical, general, historical, or interpretive as appropriate. Techniques for pond making, drainage, and the like, well covered in books already available in English, have not been included here so as to leave more room for typically Japanese treatments.

The aesthetic concepts that underlie the garden as a whole should become clear as you read through the how-to explanations in section four. Captioned color photographs are provided in the first three sections to help you develop designs, to sensitize your eye, and to give you an idea of what goes on in the garden. Look at them critically. Work through them in order, or use the index to find examples of specific garden elements that you want to study.

Give your entire garden a Japanese touch or only a corner of it, using a partition of fencing or shrubs. Or incorporate separate Japanese elements into your Western-style garden. If you live in an apartment house or work in an office, try a Japanese touch on a balcony, a porch, an area unsuitable for flowers, or even indoors. Try to use materials readily available in your area (such as mossy stones from an abandoned stone wall or curbstones to use for pavements). For your reference, the names of several dealers that will ship Japanese garden materials appear on page 79.

The recommendations in this book are drawn from the experiences of Japanese gardeners. They reflect the attitudes of the Japanese toward their landscape and are based on materials readily available in Japan (suggestions for plants and substitute materials have been provided for North American readers, however). The text's brief historical and interpretive comments should help you understand why certain materials came to be used in the Japanese garden and consequently *how* they are used and what effect they are meant to have.

The values of Zen and the tea ceremony are touched on, for they have penetrated deeply into the Japanese sense of what is good, natural, and appropriate to the environs of the home. In them are many startling approaches to garden making. There is, however, no point in worrying about whether or not your garden is "authentically Japanese." After all, it is *your* garden, and you should design it to suit your tastes. Measurements (metric; see p. 79) are given only as a guide. Imitate or innovate as you see fit; there is no sin in either.

A complete Japanese gardening manual would probably be several times the size of this book. It would also be expensive, and full of details that you would ignore anyway in the course of adapting your garden to your needs. Much gardening in Japan is done by a sense of what works and what looks best. And the key to this is your own sensitivity, drawn from your direct experience of nature. Get out to a park or woods or mountaintop and look around. Once you have an idea of the effect you want in your Japanese garden, use this book to help you achieve it.

A FEW BRIEF WORDS

The Courtyard Garden

The courtyard garden—called tsuboniwa in Japanese—is a garden in a small, enclosed area. The gardener does not fill it up; this would only congest it. Instead he carefully arranges a few items and uses their relationships to suggest more than is immediately visible to the eye. He adds manmade items like lanterns and tsukubai (water basins) to humanize the garden, to decorate it, and to allow it to function practically in daily life. He aims for balance and proportion without resorting to geometric artifice. He links the garden compositionally to his home. And he exploits numerous untouchables: wind direction, sounds, seasons, sunlight, the true and apparent dimensions of empty space.

2. A garden in an entryway. The bamboo poles of the ceiling echo the materials of the "sleeve" fence (*left*) and bring the feeling of the garden into the very entrance of the home (*right*). Note the two raised stones before the *tsukubai* and the entryway. The plant arrangement comes to life against the white wall and is changed each season—this is an autumn scene.

4. This *tsuboniwa* uses only a few elements to control vertical and horizontal dimensions. Larger stones about the base of the *tsukubai* "set" it firmly in the ground, collect overflow, and offer a size modulation. The bamboo screen in back disguises a window and functions as a one-way curtain that allows people on the other side to see into the garden.

3. This narrow garden is a design in two stages—one of stone and one of aspidistra. White sand is used to bring reflected light indoors and to brighten up the surrounding space. The round stones, black for contrast, improve drainage. Rectangular elements blend in the stepping stones and the *tsukubai*. The banana-shaped stone is a type frequently seen in gardens.

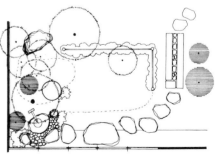

5. This garden was deliberately enclosed with a bamboo fence; a taller fence of cedar bark blocks off the property on the left. Near the *tsukubai* are scouring rushes, a common element in naturalistic gardens outdoors. Water has been liberally sprinkled to make the garden attractive, as is the custom before guests arrive. The lantern is close to the basin to provide light there in the evening.

6. When planning, the gardener always considers how the garden will appear with each season. Here, early summer colors provide a stunning accent. Squares and circles, of little-leaf box and azaleas, and vertical and diagonal tree lines form the composition. The sweeping angle of the maple (which will turn scarlet red in fall) sets the main theme and carries the garden to the porch, which extends from the house proper.

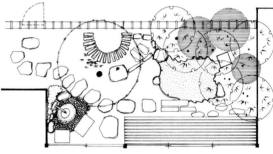

7. Many different kinds of stones taken from old buildings give this garden great charm. The pond, ringed with roof tiles, is always dry; actually it hides a drainage system. The porch supports the design from left to right and is slatted to prevent rain water from collecting. The bush at right is a Japanese aucuba.

8. A house and garden are thematically joined. Here, the horizontal and vertical lines on the sliding doors are repeated in the fence. An eave projects from the roof. The long slab links the masonry terrace with the "sea" of sand, where irregular stepping stones assert the naturalism of the garden. In the foreground is sasanqua; the green-and-white plant behind it is *Sasa veitchii*.

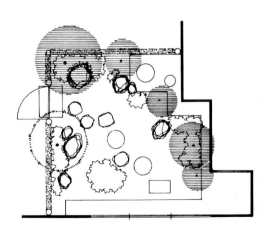

9. A fence of dried bamboo branches completely shields the garden from view without cramping it—the openwork door is an effective release here. The garden is extremely naturalistic, but stepping stones have been cut into perfect shapes for contrast. In fall and winter, red berries provide points of color.

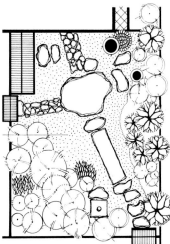

10, 11. A tea garden, viewed from the gate and the entryway. The stones—especially the one in the center that serves the three paths—are weighty in feeling, but low plantings provide needed balance to make the garden comfortable to view. The *yukimi-gata* lantern is framed by Japanese cypress, little-leaf box, and camellia. The bench by the entryway is where guests would wait prior to a tea ceremony.

12. A roof garden. It mixes Japanese and Western styles. The composition—including the surrounding architecture and pavements—is of straight lines, except for the rock, whose rough shape is enhanced by the contrast. The patch of bamboo is actually an enormous flower pot that extends almost 2 meters down, providing sufficient depth and preventing the bamboo roots from spreading.

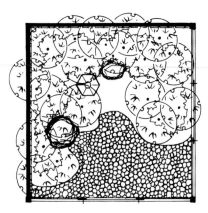

13. The irregular shape of the stone "sea" is echoed in the bank. The ferns appear agitated and contrast well with the sturdy stone lantern, which has been carefully placed to expose it fully to the viewer and to suggest a large lighthouse along the coastline.

14. Running from the gate to the entryway in the rear, the L-shaped path is the main focus of this garden, and it is given plenty of room. In the rear is a little-leaf box. Note the almost mirror-like use of stone in front that brings the outside directly into the property.

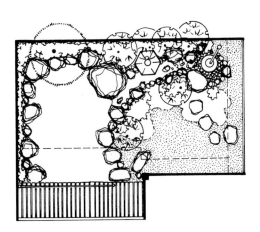

15. The massive, craggy rocks have been covered with ferns to lighten their effect. Together they represent a rocky valley. A pond lies close to the house, creating a drop that visually draws the viewer into the garden and increases its apparent size. Note the curious lantern and the overhanging eave that protects the viewer when he pauses on the bridge to admire the scene.

16–19. A garden is not static. In the spring it bursts into color and begins growing; in winter it is a still picture of repose. Sometimes the gardener adds his own touch to match the mood of the year, and in so doing celebrates the flow of nature.

Spring. The pots that contain the forsythia are disguised by baskets to suggest that the plant actually grew in the garden.

Summer. The umbrella and greenery help cool the garden on a hot day. The smoke is mosquito smudge.

Autumn. Chrysanthemums like the ones here do not grow wild in nature; unlike the spring forsythia, their pots are left exposed to view.

Winter. Tufted with snow, the garden is reduced to its essentials.

20, 21. Translucent panels form a wall that lets light in and sets off the vertical lengths of bamboo, some of which have been intentionally angled for variety. On the side of the garden is a bed for sleeping outdoors in summer. The ground cover is of moss and fallen leaves.

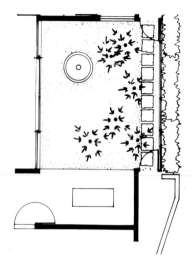

THE SOUND OF SILENCE
The Stone Garden

Within a hard stone are movement, direction, centuries of accumulated time. The gardener's task is to make these qualities visible to the human eye. He selects rough, natural stones and sets them firmly in the ground. He makes pathways and borders or suggests a waterfall, a stream, or a mountain. He may add greenery to balance or soften the stones with change and instability. And if his stones are weighty and exert a deep-rooted sense of strength and power in his garden, he says that they "live." The effect can be profound, as is realized by a character in a novel by Yasunari Kawabata: "The stone garden, weathered for centuries, had taken on such an antique patina that the stones looked as if they had always been there. However, their stiff, angular forms left no doubt that it was a human composition. . . . 'Shall we go home?' she asked. 'The stones are beginning to frighten me.' "

23. This garden uses stones in two ways—in naturalistic groupings and to suggest a stream. Every rock in the stream was carefully chosen, layered, and aligned to suggest a rapid, noisy current about to swell its banks. The moss helps tone down the effect. In front is a Japanese maple; in the rear is a Yedo hawthorn.

24. A still "lake" is bordered by rugged terrain. The flat-topped rocks at the edge help connect these two elements by unifying their shapes and suggesting a rocky beach. In the back at left is a typical *sanzon* arrangement of a waterfall; a dry stream runs down to "feed" the lake.

25. Stones are used here to express the different sounds and velocities of water as it flows from the high country to the plain. Thus, the character and sizes of the stones vary as the "stream" runs from the top right downward to the left, finally to spread out below. Azalea and creeping juniper are used for color but have taken on the shape of large stones.

26. The simplicity of the Ryoan-ji garden is deceptive. The stones of each grouping and the groupings as a whole form interlocking triangular patterns, and the power of the stones flows to the right. The design does not announce itself, but leaves the viewer composed—one of the goals of any Japanese garden. The plain wall helps unify the garden and supports the design.

27. The hedge in back mixes sasanqua and camellia and links the garden in stages to the surrounding trees. The two conical sand patterns are a curious feature, said to have developed from piles of sand originally used to replenish the garden or to spread a "carpet" for visiting nobility.

28. Interlocking ripple patterns give the "sea" great turbulence. Carefully aligned miniature hills covered with moss—it becomes green in spring—suggest a mountain range rising from the coast. The activity of both elements links them together, and the effect is not unlike that of a miniature box garden.

26

29. The stone apron is sloped for drainage and extends the line of the building to the garden, where it is then distorted—"naturalized"—by the medium-size stones that separate the moss from the sea. Note how the water basin, set into a roughly scalloped area, artfully raises the line of the stepping stones.

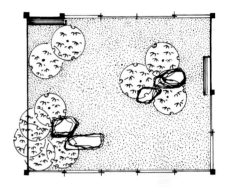

30. This simple garden recommends itself to the busy homeowner. The stones at right and left balance each other in position, height, and direction. The lithe bamboo offer contrast and, when the wind blows, sound and motion. The number of bamboo must be carefully controlled by pulling out some of the young shoots to prevent them from overpowering the stones.

31. The sand here lightens up a dark area and extends under the wooden verandah to make the garden seem larger than it is. Ripple patterns and rough stones echo each other at both ends to unify the design, and long, raked horizontals link the garden to the building. One plant in a pot or a vase of flowers would not be out of place here though.

29

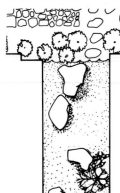

32. This garden, between two houses, was designed to hide the cap of a water-purification system. Brownish red gravel or sand is often used in private gardens instead of the more severe off-white sand of temple gardens. Originally there were more rocks in the garden, but the design was changed to the conventional triangular form shown here to decongest the space. Plantings include hydrangea, holly, and leatherleaf mahonia.

33. Gardens inside the home are generally unobtrusive. Here, bamboo shades are used to block sunlight, and bamboo in other forms is used to frame the garden on all sides. The small stepping stones are mostly decorative, but can be used to stand on when tending the greenery. Note the boxes in the ceiling that let light in from above; each box repeats the shape of the garden.

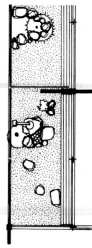

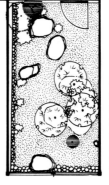

34. Bamboo are placed on small mossy mounds that look like flower pots, and many different kinds of stones are used for variety. Small stones like those against the curbing can be used to disguise a drainage pipe. The stones at the far end and the mossy mounds both form irregular triangles.

A CONSTANT MURMURING

Tree and Water Gardens

If large garden stones create solid and secure areas, then trees and water let the garden open vertically and horizontally with growth and activity. The gardener lets evergreens predominate because they suggest the constancy and endurance of nature and keep the garden green all year round. But he will add a flowering tree or one whose leaves turn brilliantly in autumn to mark seasonal change and suggest the cyclic process of all life. When he shapes trees and shrubs he does so to expose their natural character and habit, not to bend them to his will. Water is a free element, always in motion, captured only by the shape it adopts. The gardener uses it for sound. He counts its reflecting properties as a part of his design. He lets it fall, run, or gather in a pond. So important in fact is the idea of water to the garden that it will sometimes be represented by stone, gravel, or sand, in a waterless version called kare sansui.

38. Despite the size of this garden, every tree, shrub, and stone has been carefully selected and positioned. The stones are not scattered but follow the stream and lead the eye; their colors are uniform throughout. Color is provided instead by the autumn foliage, such as the single nandina with its red fruit and the bright scarlet of the enkianthus at right. This is actually a stroll garden with paths that subtly lead the viewer from one landscape to another.

36. This garden is a study in mass and movement. A shallow stream is used to make a constant gurgle; its activity contrasts well with the large little-leaf box and azalea bushes, which in turn echo the heavy stones in back. And these stones flank a thin waterfall that feeds the stream. Note how the stone tower has been partially hidden to give a sense of mystery to the scene.

37. This is but one section of a much larger garden. The stream is shallow so that the small stones in the bed are visible and become part of the design. Hammered-in posts with lilies support the bank. The flat rock can be used for sitting.

39. Water is often used, as here, for its open, reflective properties. The small pine suggests that the rocks might be large crags in a vast lake or islands in an ocean. Stones should be set in water, as they are in soil, to look stable. Often more than half their bulk is below the water line.

Little-leaf box.

Azalea.

Azalea.

Little-leaf box.

Little-leaf box, azalea, maple, sasanqua.

40–45. The gardener methodically shapes trees and bushes for contrast, to link the garden with manmade elements like the house or a stone lantern, and to express the quality of the site. Shaping interprets the plant, drawing from its many different properties those which best suit the garden.

Azalea, little-leaf box.

From the studio.

From the wooden bridge, looking toward the Wisdom Stone.

46–49. The sculptor Fumio Asakura (1883–1964) made this garden for the 160-square-meter tract between his studio and his home. Mindful of the artist's need for order and discernment and wary of the hardening of the spirit that comes with age and public recognition, Asakura designed his garden to stimulate reflections on the principles by which good men live. Five large stones denote the Five Confucian Virtues, and white-flowered trees bloom throughout the year to suggest the purity of life from birth to death. To suggest imperfection, there is a single red crape myrtle. The design presents a balanced arrangement no matter what direction it is viewed from.

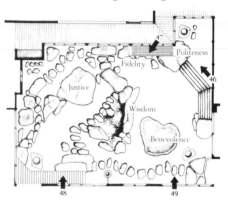

From the main house, looking toward the Justice Stone.

From the guest room, looking toward the fountain.

GRAMMAR AND VOCABULARY
The Language of the Japanese Garden

A garden, be it Western or Japanese, is like speech; it is an expression with intention and design. The gardener selects plantings and ornaments that please him, and he arranges them by whatever criteria he feels are important; he may favor function over shape, or color over texture. He is practical and accumulates information before deciding anything; he checks the pH of his soil, studies the climate, investigates drainage problems, considers the needs of his household, figures costs, and estimates the time required for maintenance. On these counts, Western and Japanese gardeners are much the same. Yet the languages their gardens speak are different. This section takes up the language of the Japanese garden—its words, which are its stones, streams, and plants, and its grammar, which is the system of arrangement that carries the message.

A BASIS FOR COMMUNICATION

Two Courtyard Gardens

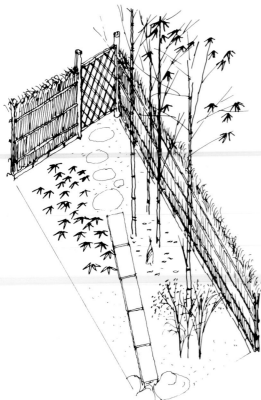

The possibilities in a single space are infinite. The gardener selects according to his taste, the climate of the area, soil conditions, and his understanding of the spatial relationships that govern the garden. Small gardens require careful planning because in a tiny area the slightest flaw, overgrowth, clutter, or imbalance will be magnified in effect.

The Japanese garden is nature on a microcosmic scale. This is not to say that it is nature imitated; rather it is nature symbolized and represented. By laying in a "grammatical" structure, the gardener develops linked patterns with concise natural forms. These in turn suggest their own essences and fill with meaning.

Straight lines and perfect geometric shapes like circles and squares are rarely used except for contrast or to echo the lines of a nearby building.

Asymmetrical designs and odd-numbered groupings are favored. Not being evenly divisible, these prevent the garden from having a sense of completion and suggest the wildness of nature.

Contrast is very important. For example, a whole row of red flowers is not used, only a single red flower in a swell of green. Trees are varied in a group—flowering trees, evergreens, deciduous trees, and trees with interesting branch patterns are placed together.

The gardener suggests the passage of time by building change and motion into the garden. Trees are selected for their properties in different seasons, and fluid water-forms are contrasted with stable stones.

Much as in Japanese ink-painting, "white areas" of empty space are left in the garden for balance and to allow room for the viewer's imagination to wander.

A busy garden too full of movement or color calls undue attention to its separate parts. The gardener aims for a total effect wherein all elements are balanced to suggest quietude and repose.

Everything superfluous to the total effect of the garden is discarded. The gardener's design is complete when there is nothing more he can *remove* from the garden.

There is no vista. The garden does not have a single view but many views, each one appearing as one moves through the garden or walks around it. The ideal garden is like an unrolling picture scroll that prompts surprise at every turn. But a small garden will usually have one central focus and one theme that is developed by the surrounding elements.

A moist look is favored, probably because of the great amount of precipitation in Japan. Gardens look best after a rain, for wettening brings out the natural patina of stone and deepens the mood of the observer.

The garden is a study in relationships. When planning, the gardener is concerned with the interaction of every part—slopes, colors, sounds, shapes, and movements. He enforces these interactions by artful placement, by using branches as frames, and by playing with perspective techniques to lengthen and bend dimensions. The shadings he adds have an almost palpable relationship and resonate through every element of the garden.

Actually, the garden's intricate and deep structure is really just a shell. For in the end, the garden speaks for itself. The length of shadows in winter, the seed pods that carpet the ground in spring, and the direction and sound of the wind are some of the many things the gardener can't control. He doesn't try to. They are as much a part of the design of his garden as the rock or lantern. By giving nature its freedom, the gardener opens himself to the new relationships that nature will suggest.

LAYOUT: WHERE DO I PUT THE ROCK?

The factors to consider when planning the Japanese garden are: location, size and shape, function, style of composition, use of space, and materials. Each of these is a part of the language of the garden, and none can be considered separate from the others. But it makes sense to treat them in stages, if only to limit the information you have to contend with at any given time. The following discussion takes up the case of a typical homeowner who has found a large, moss-covered stone that he wants to use as the focus of his garden. The illustrations show a simple technique for developing an asymmetrical structure, for deciding the lay of the garden, and for finding the best place to put the stone (or whatever you decide will be the focus of your garden).

1   The gardener makes a sketch of his property. He draws in his terrace and makes hash lines for windows to show all the places from which the garden might be viewed. He indicates north. He shows on his drawing all the elements on the site or around it that might affect his composition. He notes activities within the home.

The gardener then selects the northeast corner of his property for the garden, mostly because he wants it to be visible both from the terrace and from the living and dining rooms, where guests visit. He decides to put in a fence to block off the tool shed (which he needs) and to give his children a place to play. He assumes that it will be a low bamboo fence so that light from the south is not blocked off and the shadow is not too long in winter.

2   The gardener draws a blowup of the garden space. To break the regular rectangle into asymmetric sections he draws a nine-block grid (if the garden were longer he would have used four lines to make a fifteen-block grid). The four circled points are strong points; one of them will take the stone.

3   To cut costs and make his work easier, the gardener decides to leave one section of the garden virtually empty in contrast to a main section he will fill. To increase the apparent size of the garden, he decides to place the main section as far from the vantage point on the terrace as possible. But he also wants his garden to be seen from the windows in the dining and living rooms. He wants to accommodate his neighbor's trees, which are grand and full. And he wants the trees he plants to turn their flowers toward the house in springtime. So he draws a line as shown. The shaded area will be the main section of the garden. Not incidentally, he has also found the point to lay the stone. Note that it is not centered either in relation to the main section or to the garden as a whole.

4   The gardener sets the stone in the design with its front toward the terrace. To discover the proper arrangement of other elements in the garden he collects household items of different heights and shapes (candlesticks, playing cards, bowls) and experiments on a table top with different configurations. When he finds an arrangement suited to the space—balanced horizontally and vertically—he translates that design into materials that suit his theme.

5   The gardener makes a sketch of his garden. In the course of actually laying things out, checking materials, and deciding on specific plantings, his design may change. He may discard it completely. But at least he has something to go on and a good understanding of the character of his site.

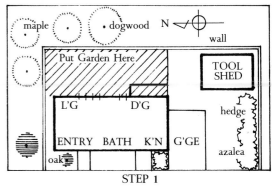

STEP 1

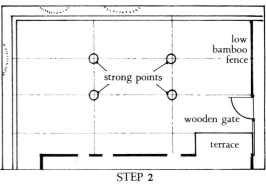

STEP 2

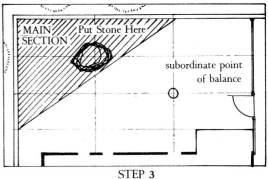

STEP 3

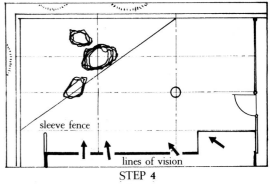

STEP 4

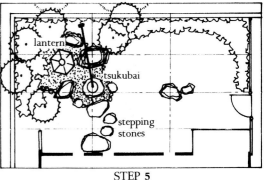

STEP 5

STONE GROUPINGS

52. This stone resembles a ship at sea.

51. Leaning the stone has energized this design.

53. In a glade, a balanced *sanzon* grouping.

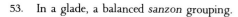

54. Squat stones provide stability in the garden.

Severe yet provocative, stone groupings symbolize the rugged landscape. Balanced in design, they counterpoint the vigorous play of the seasons.

55. This arrangement evokes the hills with abstract shapes.

56. Growths on stones give depth and soften the lines.

57. A bridge supports the design in back.

59. "Water" cascades down a long mountain valley.

58. Here, a deep, rugged gorge.

STONE GROUPINGS

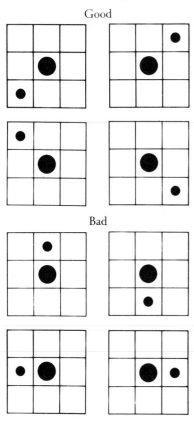

Two-Stone Arrangements

Good

Bad

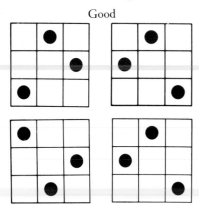

Three-Stone Arrangements

Good

All the stones are of different size

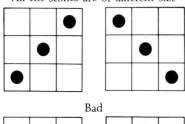

Bad

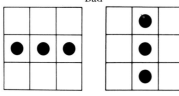

The versatility of stone is clearly displayed in the most famous temple garden in Japan, that of the Ryoan-ji in the old capital city of Kyoto (see the photograph on page 26). Fifteen rather ordinary stones in five groupings rest on a bed of off-white gravel in a closed courtyard. The composition is provocative, but no records exist to tell us what the designer meant by it.

One theory, apparently linked to Confucian teachings, says that the Ryoan-ji garden is an imaginative, life-size stone painting of tigers and their cubs swimming across a river. Another theory interprets the garden as a miniature but true-form representation of a natural vista in which islands dot a vast sea or mountains poke above the clouds. But many commentators reject such rationalizing, saying that the garden is to be appreciated solely for its abstract quality—the dynamic balance attained through the character and placement of each element. In this last view may lie the basis for the garden's curiously modern appeal.

The stones, of course, are indifferent to the controversy, as perhaps we should be, for Japanese garden makers throughout history have consciously used stones in all three of the ways mentioned above. One finds realistic stone constructions of cranes and tortoises or natural, miniature representations of waterfalls, sacred Buddhist islands, crags, and mountains. One finds, too, artful arrangements seeming to propose nothing more than that disparate shapes can be linked to create a unified space.

No matter what purpose they are used for, stones in a Japanese garden are never inorganic lumps of functionless matter. Ancient Shinto animistic beliefs led the Japanese to see certain stones as the abodes of gods and to festoon them with straw ropes to sanctify the forces within. It may not be wholly inappropriate to use a modern term and say that what the early animists celebrated in the stones was their "gravity," an invisible but actual force. The Ryoan-ji garden is a more elaborate vision; its stones interact, attract each other, so perfectly that not one can be removed without unbalancing the entire composition. You can get good results in your own garden by learning to exploit this radiant power that "bends," that participates in, the empty space beyond the surface of the stone.

Not just any stone is used in the Japanese garden. Uncut stones that show the effects of weathering are favored and have special qualities related to the areas from which they came; they may have been smoothed or roughly polished by rivers or oceans or been eaten away by violent winds and storms. Their color may have "settled" to give calmness and stability. Rocks with growths of rust or moss are especially prized. Round and square stones are not used; nor are mechanically polished stones, which have lost the patina of age. The best colors are subdued shades of greenish blue, brown, red, or purple. White stones lack interest, and distracting color clashes should be avoided.

A stone has joints and angles which work together to suggest a direction in which its strength naturally seems to flow. Garden makers with long experience can walk around a stone and immediately determine which side is the "front" or "face," that is, which side is to be presented to the viewer of the garden. Discover the physical, internal qualities of a stone by first determining where its center of gravity lies; then imagine successively higher ground lines along the face of the stone to see how the apparent center of gravity will move when the rock is buried in the soil.

Design Principles. Stones provide the most stable element of a design. The *Sakuteiki*, a gardening manual from 11th-century Japan, discusses in detail the proper placement of stones, and even warns that bad positioning may bring bad fortune to the inept designer. This warning should not be taken lightly even today. Correcting mistakes in the placements of stones is hard work, and having to move one stone may involve moving all of them; this is bad fortune indeed. Select stones only after you have decided how and where you will use them. Fill a plastic garbage bag with air and tie off sections with rubber bands to make "stones" for testing shapes and placements.

If there are more than two stones, the customary arrangement is in odd-numbered groups of three, five, or seven. Such groupings are often broken into subgroups of twos and threes; thus, if seven stones are used they will be in clusters of three, two, and two stones or two, three, and two stones. The triangular grouping with one tall central stone and two smaller ones flanking it for balance—called *sanzon*—is a traditional arrangement often used to represent a waterfall. The form is derived from the Buddhist trinity; its religious implications aside, it allows the Japanese gardener to formalize nature without making it look artificial. There is, in any case, no need for rigidity. Groups exceeding three stones can use several stones in combination to make one vertex or can be thought of as an overlaying of several triangles on the same site. And sometimes a vertex may be omitted entirely, to be mentally supplied by the viewer during contemplation.

Strive for variety. Do not place rocks of the same height, shape, or mass next to each other. Give the natural qualities of stone their freedom. Do not force a rugged mountain stone into the role of a smooth one collected from a stream or seaside. A stone grouping, even if it is to be the main point of interest, should be placed a bit off to the side of the garden. Against a back wall it may make the garden look cramped; but if placed a bit forward of the midline it will help expand the perception of distance to the rear.

Some typical arrangments of two and three stones are shown here. Note that stones are always on a diagonal. The base of the entire formation is usually parallel (or nearly parallel) to the front of the garden, and all the stones have their powers aligned to flow in the same direction.

Setting. Much of the bulk of a stone is often hidden beneath the soil. The stone appears to have been in the garden forever and to be spreading outward below the ground. Stones whose bases angle in to the ground or that look as if they are about to fall over create a tension that detracts from the stable qualities favored in the garden. Where proper placement is impossible, disguise the "defect" with shrubbery or grass. Plantings in soil packed between or around stones need plenty of water in summer to prevent their baking from the stones' radiant heat.

Stones can also be set in a pond by constructing a platform for them of smaller stones or bricks. Think of the surface of the water as the ground line and set the stone accordingly.

Triangular Arrangements

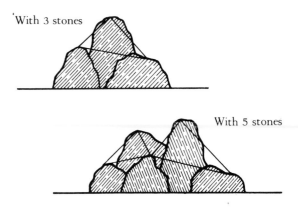

With 3 stones

With 5 stones

Setting Stones in Soil and Water

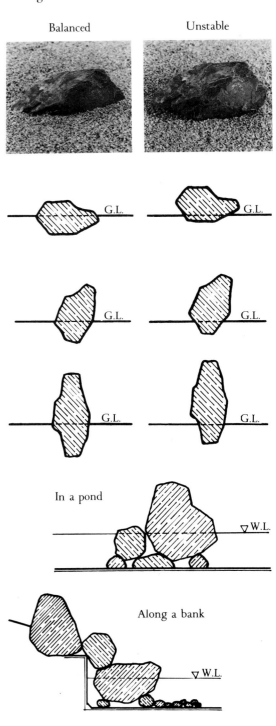

Balanced Unstable

G.L.

In a pond

Along a bank

STEPPING STONES,
STONE PAVEMENTS, SAND GARDENS

60. The path bends as a lantern comes into view.

61. These stones are related in shape, but not identical.

62. Stones are sometimes almost completely buried.

63. Perfect and natural shapes create a comfortable tension.

64. Turning shapes and using moss add variety.

65. The straight line is countered by irregular stones.

66. Four-point junctions are meticulously avoided.

67. A regular path ends abruptly in a sea of moss.

Stepping stones and pavements must be built with people in mind. Controlling speed and perspective, they can determine whether a garden is appreciated or merely observed. For sand gardens, see page 47.

68. Wet stones deepen this garden's mood.

69. Wooden slats suggest a bridge in a dense forest.

STEPPING STONES, STONE PAVEMENTS, SAND GARDENS

Stepping Stones. Stepping stones in gardens were developed by 16th-century tea-ceremony masters to make the approaches to their tea rooms practical and attractive. Guests invited to the ceremony would first wait in an adjoining garden and then, when summoned by their host, file through an inner garden to the tea room. By the time they reached the tea room, the guests were expected to have attained the level of mental refinement necessary for them to partake fully of the ceremony's delicate, careful atmosphere. The tea garden was thus the first stage of the tea ceremony, and every element in it was designed to discourage distractions and promote inner harmony.

Stepping stones still contribute to the overall effect of the garden. Preventing upsets on slippery moss or soiling of footwear and kimono (or long dresses), they offer a firm surface for walking leisurely and without concern. They also contribute an aesthetic element; there is no unsightly worn and muddy path, and the usual asymmetric arrangement of the stones suggests the naturalism of the rest of the garden. And, since a guest naturally walks along the stones and nowhere else, the path is a means by which a host can unobtrusively present appealing views for appreciation.

Use cut stones or uncut, flat-topped stones buried deep in the soil. The long axis of each stone should be perpendicular to the path; where the path turns, the pivot stone's axle should bend in the same direction. Follow concave shapes with convex ones (and vice versa), and flat edges with flat edges to give the path a continuous flow. Mixing and matching the stones until the path is right is often a matter of trial and error, but the work will proceed quickly once your eye is trained. The farther apart the stones, the quicker one tends to walk, and the closer together, the slower. Always think of what the walker will see before him on the path and strive to create points of interest and places to pause.

Stepping stones can also be laid in water. Make them easy to walk on and anchor them firmly, in concrete if necessary.

Stone Pavements. Pavements of cut stones in regular shapes were a later development in Japanese gardens and are often seen today. They are particularly pleasing in a wide, open stretch where they will not clash with the naturalism and asymmetry of typical garden elements. But even in narrow spaces, contemporary Japanese designers have learned to fuse the inherent geometry of the stones with a rough naturalism, creating a pleasing modernity that links the Western-style building with the garden and refashions traditional values without fragmenting them. Some artifice is generally used, too, to upset the regularity of the stones: four-point intersections are avoided, shapes and sizes are varied, and moss or low plantings are inserted here and there between the stones.

In general, the larger the stones the more space between them. About 10 mm. is sufficient spacing for bricks and small stones. If the stones are thick the joints should be deep and not filled in with soil. You may have to pack in mortar with thin stones to prevent slippage. Slate is readily available, but any material can be used: natural or manmade stone, bricks, even concrete. Add variety by using a large, flat, natural stone as a pivot.

Patterns for Stepping Stones

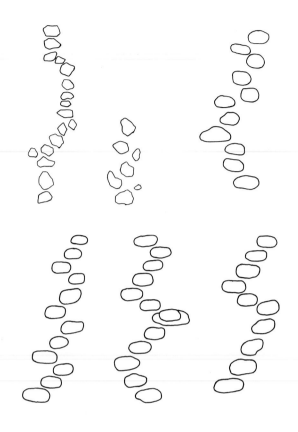

Patterns for Pavements

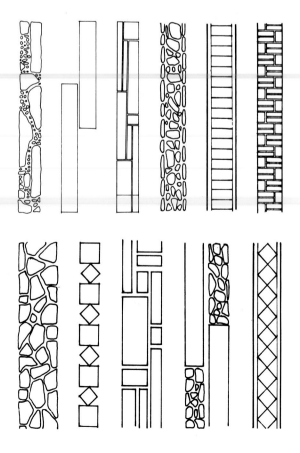

Sand Gardens.   The "sand" used in Japanese gardens is not beach sand but a granitic, decomposed gravel that accumulates at the bases of cliffs through weathering and erosion. This sand comes in varying shades of white and gray with reddish brown or black specks. Particles are usually about 2 mm. in diameter. The grits fed to turkeys and hens by poultry farmers in the United States are just the right size. Sand was used early on in garden making to prevent the feet from getting muddied. In later years, sand's laconic purity was exploited by Zen masters, who developed gardens based on philosophical themes. Sand in the garden today most often represents a body of water and has ripple and wave patterns raked into its surface to heighten the effect.

Sand is an austere, fragile material, and most sand gardens are necessarily wind-free enclosures designed for viewing. They achieve spaciousness in small areas, but they are not very suitable for daily activity. You may find it more practical to use sand only in one section of the garden with a brick or stone edging, around bamboo to highlight the verticality of the trunks, or around other plantings to prevent unwanted growth and make maintenance easier. Avoid using sand near lawn grass; its grains will damage the delicate blades. Light-colored sand in sunny places will produce a blinding glare, but it will brighten up a garden indoors or on the north side of the house.

Sand is spread on tamped earth to a depth of 5–6 cm. Prevent muddiness by spreading a thin layer of concrete over the ground before you add the sand; slant it for drainage. (Simpler yet, lay down vinyl sheeting and punch holes in it.) Evergreens work best in the sand garden. They provide much-needed contrast all year round and create fewer maintenance problems; leaves of deciduous trees will fall in autumn and have to be picked from the sand one by one.

Some examples of sand patterns are shown on this page. A pattern will usually remain in the sand for two weeks under good weather conditions. Spray water on the sand to enhance its beauty, and add new sand periodically to replace that which has been lost to settling or heavy winds.

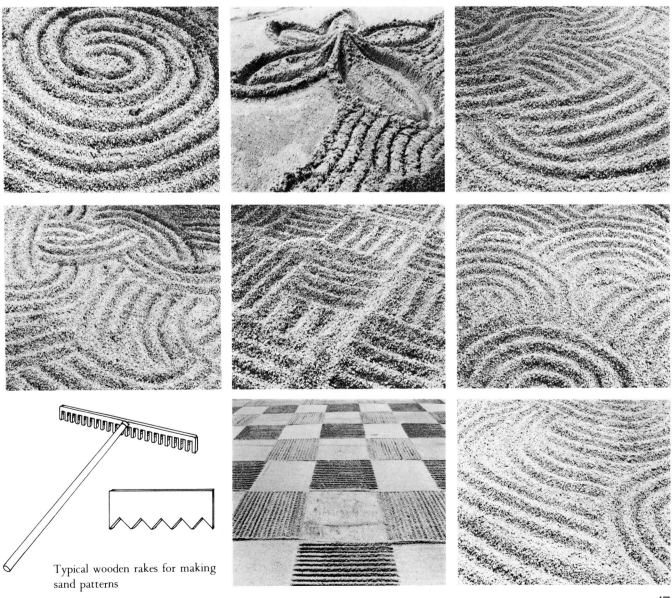

Typical wooden rakes for making sand patterns

47

STONE LANTERNS, STONE TOWERS, STONE BUDDHAS, SIGNPOSTS

Stone ornaments look manmade. But this lets them humanize the garden with tasteful decoration. And by providing light, directions, or a place to worship, they help the garden function in daily life.

70. An *oki-gata* lantern.

71. A *tachi-gata* lantern.

72. A *tachi-gata* lantern.

73. A *yukimi-gata* lantern.

74. A *yukimi-gata* lantern.

75. An *ikekomi-gata* lantern.

76. An *oki-gata* lantern.

77. An *oki-gata* lantern.

78. A thirteen-story stone tower.

79. A tower with a carved pedestal.

81. A signpost at a fork in a path.

80. A stone Buddha.

STONE LANTERNS, STONE TOWERS, STONE BUDDHAS, SIGNPOSTS

Stone Lanterns.   Stone lanterns, like stepping stones, were introduced into the Japanese garden by tea masters. Tea ceremonies were often held in the evening, and light had to be provided to guide the guests through the garden to the tea room. Nowadays lanterns are primarily for decoration, but their older light-giving function is still retained in that they are never placed where light would not be needed. Conventional placements are therefore at the turn in a path, on the edge of a pond or stream, near a bridge, or near the *tsukubai* (water basin; see pp. 52–55). A lantern is usually the principal element of its group, with smaller stones scattered about to balance the height. Sometimes a tree is placed in back with a single branch trained to hang over the top of the lantern.

Early lanterns were based on the designs of hanging temple lanterns and were made of bronze. That the Japanese gradually came to favor stone and wood constructions shows their love for natural, plain materials with rugged shapes. Soft stone of rough texture has the most favored appearance but is easily damaged by weathering. Harder stone can be used, but it is difficult to handle and cut and consequently more expensive. Lanterns made of synthetic resins find frequent use on roof tops or balconies that cannot support much weight. Though less expensive than natural stone, the manmade materials are distinctly inferior in radiant mass and feeling; an experienced eye can soon tell the difference. If excess weight might be a problem in your garden, consider using a lantern made of very lightweight pumice or even building one of wood. Concrete, cast-formed lanterns are available, but since your garden probably needs just one lantern, why make it a factory piece that lacks distinction?

Lanterns come in many different styles, some based on lanterns in Buddhist temples and others developed by tea masters for their own gardens, the Rikyu, Oribe, Enshu, Kasuga, and Sowa styles being particularly well known. Lanterns can be classified as follows:

Tachi-gata (pedestal lanterns): These are used mainly in large gardens and commonly stand about 1½ meters high, though sometimes run up to 3 meters. Lanterns of this size have quite an overpowering effect and naturally become the focus of the entire garden. Both space problems and the cost of stone have contributed to their disappearance from the gardens of private residences.

Ikekomi-gata (buried lanterns): These lack a pedestal because the shaft is inserted directly into the ground. They are often used near the *tsukubai* but look good anywhere in the garden.

Oki-gata (small, set lanterns): Most often, these are found on the edge of a pond, at the side of a path, or in very small courtyard gardens. Tiny and relatively unobtrusive, they can be used with a light touch.

Yukimi-gata (snow-viewing lanterns): These are the most popular form and are used near water elements. Their low postures and open-leg designs give them a breezy intimacy that is well appreciated in a small area. They are so named because of the delicate way they hold snow on the roof; hexagonal and round roofs are both available.

As with all aspects of garden making, you are advised to select for simplicity. An elaborate lantern with intricate embellishment is

A Tachi-gata Stone Lantern, Balanced by a Tree and a Rock

Cap
Roof
Lamp housing
Housing support
Shaft
Pedestal

Types of Lanterns

Tachi-gata lanterns

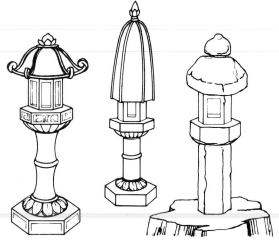

Ikekomi-gata lanterns

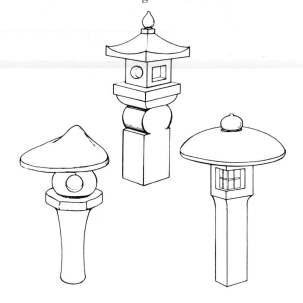

Oki-gata lantern

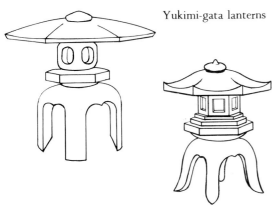

Yukimi-gata lanterns

Stone Tower

Signpost

Stone Buddha

a hard act to follow and doesn't go very well with anything a normal homeowner can afford. If you look hard around your area you may even be able to find stones that you can arrange as a makeshift lantern. Think of your lantern as being "rustic" rather than "crude" if you are worried about its not looking right.

You should consider using a lantern at night to illuminate only a few points in the garden rather than bathing the entire area with a floodlamp. Turn the face of the flamebox toward the viewing area or the *tsukubai*, or position it to throw light on a rock formation or along a path. A lantern light glimmering through leaves strikes just the right mood on a summer's night. Many people today use electric illumination inside the flamebox, but you may find a candle far superior in effect and easier to install. Paper or frosted-glass panels may be used to soften the light.

Lanterns (and other tall structures) should sit atop stone-and-concrete footings that extend below the frost line. Set a pedestal lantern directly atop the footing and pack in dirt halfway up the edge of the base. Make the footing for a buried lantern shorter so that you can sink the shaft a good distance into the ground. Make sure the lantern is plumb; for added stability, use bricks, tiles, or a board set flush against the shaft in the hole.

Stone Towers. Stone towers, derived from Indian stupas, are a purely decorative element in the garden today, but in earlier times were used to add a spiritual atmosphere. There is always an odd number of stories, and the plates are most often square, though hexagonal, octagonal, and round ones are also seen. For a small garden, a five-story tower should be quite sufficient.

Placement of the stone tower is very similar to that of the lantern. Near *tsukubai*, bridges, ponds, and streams, towers work especially well, not only because of the artful contrast of vertical and horizontal elements but also because they put the reflecting properties of water to good use. Taller towers are often seen atop artificial miniature hills and ground swellings. Towers do not work as well against thin elements that compete for the viewer's attention, but they look good against fences, near bulky ornamental stones, and beside thick-trunked trees. Tucked away in a grove they can suggest a mountain temple.

Stone Buddhas. Small figures of Buddhist gods have long been used as objects of worship and are frequently found in gardens within temple compounds. Most figures seen in private gardens are reproductions, and while not sacred relics do at least reflect the religious inclinations of the household, much as the statue of Jesus or the Holy Mother does in some Western gardens. Tasteful use is therefore in order, if not for the sake of the stone Buddha then as a sign of respect to those millions who believe in its efficacy. Set it firmly in an inconspicuous place and leave it unhighlighted. The standard height is about 40–50 cm.

Signposts. Signposts are placed in a conspicuous part of the garden and can serve as a replacement for the stone lantern. They are often seen on the edges of garden paths or within low, planted areas. Placed at a turn or fork in a path, a signpost telling what lies to the right and left can be a tasteful way of guiding visitors through the garden. In Japan, directions are given in carved characters and script that read vertically from the top down.

TSUKUBAI, SHISHI ODOSHI

A store of water is kept in the garden in honor of an old ritual of purification. A man stands up after drinking and hears the clack of bamboo; the sound penetrates the garden and fades. Time is moving on.

82. A typical *tsukubai*, well integrated with its site.

83. Tall basins are sometimes set near the house.

84. The pieces of bamboo on top are to support the ladle.

85. The basin's lines are not parallel to the house.

86. A lantern is nearby for illumination.

87. The round basin contrasts with the rough stones.

88. An artificial element, the *shishi odoshi* is roughly built.

90. The water from this *shishi odoshi* feeds into the stream.

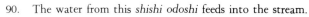

89. This basin stone carefully echoes the lantern behind.

TSUKUBAI, SHISHI ODOSHI

Tsukubai. The *tsukubai*, or water basin, is yet another contribution of the tea masters to Japanese garden design. Guests were expected to enter the tea room pure in mind and body. To this end, the tea master provided a garden to relax the spirit and a pitcher of water for hand washing. This pitcher developed into the *tsukubai*, and the layouts shown on this page are two of the many that have become established over the years.

The low height of the conventional *tsukubai*—between 20–30 cm.—may seem inconvenient. This is quite intentional, for the low height helped induce humility among those about to attend the tea ceremony by making them stoop while washing (thus the name, from the word *tsukubau*, "to bend or crouch"). The tops of some *tsukubai* are even placed flush with the ground. Basins standing 50–60 cm. tall are not unusual, however.

When natural stone is used for the basin a hole with a wide diameter (12–30 cm. depending on the stone) is bored into the top. The stone is then placed on the edge of a "sea," which collects overflow or catches the water that falls during hand washing. There is always a flat stone on which to stand in front. To the left and right are stones slightly smaller than the basin stone; on these one lays down objects while washing or places a hot-water pitcher for use in the winter.

In place of natural stone one often sees millstones, foundation stones that once held building pillars, and the pedestals or shafts of lanterns and towers. By using old, manmade objects the gardener stirs recollections of past lifestyles; this adds to the strain of inevitability in the garden and deepens the sense of time's passage. These stones, usually low and of regular shape, are placed in the center of the sea, on a platform if necessary. A perfect rectangular block may have a corner chipped away to give it an appealing imperfection.

Unfortunately, one can rarely demand purity and humility from one's guests anymore, but this does not mean that the *tsukubai* need be merely decorative. After working in the garden you can wash your hands there. The water in the basin can be sprinkled over the garden to give it a fresh appearance. If you do not attach a drain you can use the overflow as a source of a small stream. And the design itself, in addition to providing visual interest, can, when placed near the home, suggest a strong link between the foundation of the home and the stones or other water elements in the garden. Place a wooden ladle atop the basin so that you can take out water at any time.

There are no fixed rules for the location of the *tsukubai*. Its placement will depend on the overall layout of the garden and on whether you intend to use it often as a source of water. It generally looks best in a low or wide, flat area before a stone wall, bamboo fence, or hedge toward the back. As a rule, separate the *tsukubai* from waterfalls and wells because the two strong water elements will compete for attention. Set a stone lantern nearby for vertical balance and nighttime illumination.

CONSTRUCTION: When the *tsukubai* is placed on the edge of the sea, it is in the center rear, the sea is below and in front, and the flat rock on which a person stands while washing is a bit higher than

Tsukubai with Basin on Edge of Sea

Cross-section of layout

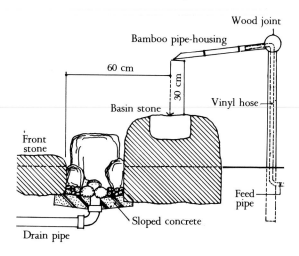

Front view

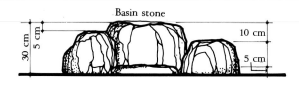

Top view

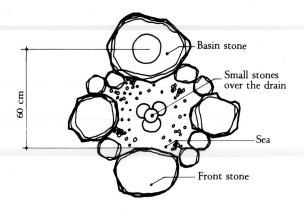

Cross-section of basin stone

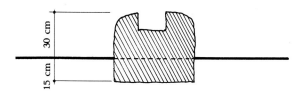

Tsukubai with Basin in Center of Sea

Top view

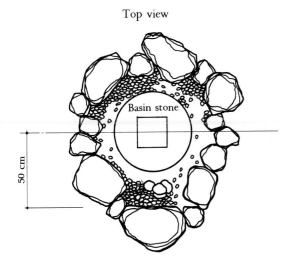

50 cm

Basin stone

Cross-section of basin stone and rocks

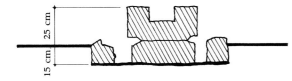

25 cm

15 cm

Shishi Odoshi

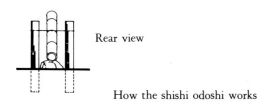

Rear view

How the shishi odoshi works

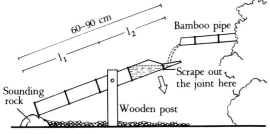

60–90 cm

l_2

l_1

Bamboo pipe

Scrape out the joint here

Sounding rock

Wooden post

1. Water collects

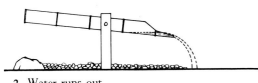

2. Water runs out

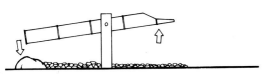

3. The bamboo strikes the sounding rock

the stepping stones that usually lead up to it. The two larger, round rocks on the left and right balance each other.

First determine where the front of the basin will be. Set the basin stone so that its top is 20–30 cm. above ground level. Much of the stone is buried; follow the same principles here as for setting stones arranged in groups (see pp. 40–43). Then anchor the three large rocks in the soil in front around the sea. Dig the sea to a depth of about 15 cm.; install a drain in the center if you do not want the water to collect there.

Now add smaller rocks to connect the large stones; set them with mortar if necessary. Lay a thin layer of concrete in the bed of the sea, sloping it so that all the water will run into the drain. Pile rocks about 7–8 cm. in diameter to hide the drain hole, and in the bed of the sea scatter pebbles that are 2–3 cm. in diameter. Add plantings of grass and ferns after packing earth around the rocks forming the circumference of the sea.

The construction technique is similar for the other configurations. For a *tsukubai* in the center of a sea, place it on a platform to adjust its height. Make sure it is level so that water overflows on all sides. Arrange flat rocks and lower, rounder rocks about the circumference of the sea. Fill in the sea with small pebbles into which overflow will seep and disappear. A drain is optional. Large *tsukubai* that don't overflow can be set without a surrounding sea if they are of excellent design, or next to the home atop sturdy platforms.

To supply water to the basin, run a copper or PVC pipe or a vinyl hose from the house supply, either underground or hidden behind plantings. Attach lengths of bamboo to the sections of the hose above the ground. Add water to the basin when needed or feed it slowly in a narrow stream or regular drip to produce a constant overflow. Sometimes water is fed up from the floor of the basin. If you don't want to do any plumbing work, periodically hand-carry new water to the basin and clean it regularly to prevent it from appearing stagnant.

Shishi Odoshi. The *shishi odoshi*, or "deer scare," was originally developed by farmers as a means of scaring off deer and wild boar that damaged their crops. Water is fed through a thin bamboo pipe into an angled length of thick bamboo which is set on an axle and whose first joint has been scraped or cut away on the inside. Water collects, and its weight forces the front tip of the bamboo to the ground; when the water runs out, the rear end of the bamboo, now heavier than the tip, drops quickly to the ground, where it strikes against a rock to produce a sharp, clacking sound. The flow of water and the regular movement of the *shishi odoshi* provide an effective counterpoint to the changelessness of the other garden elements. The sudden clack of the bamboo and its resonant dissolution suggest to some the process and effects of time.

The *shishi odoshi* is often placed on the edge of a pond, which serves to collect the water that runs off. It can also be used on slightly higher ground as a source of a stream or waterfall.

STREAMS, WATERFALLS, SHORE PROTECTIONS, BRIDGES

Japan is surrounded by the sea, and tiny brooks clutter its deep-mountain landscapes. Water in the garden helps offset the weight of stone and provides melody, movement, and open, reflective zones.

92. This stream represents a mountain brook.

91. Rocks at the base are used for sound.

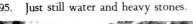

93. Stones flank this rapid falls for stability.

95. Just still water and heavy stones. 96. Wooden posts support the bank. 97. Stones create a desolate shore.

98. Bridges and stepping stones are mixed here.

94. A multitude of visual and sound patterns.

99. Stones for walking are placed close together in water.

100. The regularity of this bridge is forceful.

102. Thick planks echo the strong stones.

101. Sharp turns deftly control the walker's view.

STREAMS, WATERFALLS, SHORE PROTECTIONS, BRIDGES

Stream Configurations

Side views

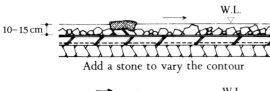

10–15 cm

Add a stone to vary the contour

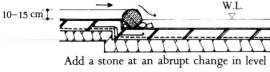

10–15 cm

Add a stone at an abrupt change in level

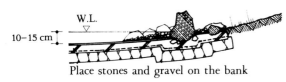

10–15 cm

Place stones and gravel on the bank

Front views

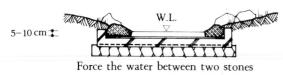

5–10 cm

Force the water between two stones

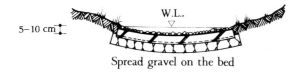

5–10 cm

Spread gravel on the bed

Waterfall Configurations

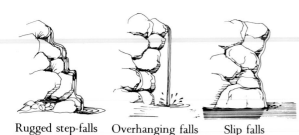

Rugged step-falls   Overhanging falls   Slip falls

Two-story falls   Curtain falls

Regular step-falls   Ribbon falls

Water has always been a part of the Japanese garden. In the Heian period (ca. 8th–12th centuries), spacious gardens with ponds and islets based on Chinese models were constructed by the aristocracy, and members of the court would board dragon-shaped boats and move leisurely through the gardens, admiring the various views and, we imagine, exchanging tasteful conversation. Under the influence of Zen Buddhism, gardeners built many dry-landscape gardens, but even here they suggested the rush of water by assembled-stone compositions or raked sand patterns. Water in the garden today provides fluidity, sound, and motion and helps offset the immobility and heaviness of stone.

Water is also reflective, less dense than stone. A tower or lantern placed for reflection on the edge of a pond can do double duty and help to increase the garden's apparent size. Sunlight reflected from the water's surface can brighten up a room where overhanging eaves or branches would otherwise place it in the shade.

But water's active qualities must be well adapted to the garden. A tall waterfall in the corner of a spacious garden, for example, is perfectly in scale; the same waterfall would be too strong in the foreground of a small courtyard. If the garden is near the bedroom, the best configuration lets the waterfall slip smoothly over the rocks rather than plunging noisily into a pool. Too much movement in the garden can be unsettling; keep devices like the *shishi odoshi* to a minimum.

Streams. Because most people can no longer make use of natural water sources like wells and springs, gardens these days have filtering and circulating mechanisms to provide a constant supply of clean water at low cost. If you use such a system, make sure it is absolutely leak free. Keep the stream shallow so that the contour of the flow can be effectively dramatized with stones in the bed. The slope of the stream is usually about 3%, and you can increase the speed of the flow by using two rocks that force the water to narrow and run quickly between them. In most cases the part of the stream nearest the building or viewing area is widest; for a backyard garden about 1 meter here is sufficient. Lay a thin layer of concrete to shape the bed of the stream and to prevent it from settling.

Plants that do not grow rampant or high may be placed alongside or in the stream, alone or with small rock formations. Stones can also be used where the stream turns or where the flow is quick to prevent the bank from being worn away (see also "Shore Protections," below). Some possible layouts are illustrated on this page. In these configurations you can use small stones in place of flowing water to make a dry landscape (*kare sansui*). Depending on the size, quality, and direction of the stones, the dry stream can represent anything from a lazy mountain brook to a flashing torrent.

Heian-period designers directed the course of the stream under the building, which was raised a bit higher than normal to prevent flood damage. If you are thinking of remodeling or of adding on to your home, you might consider such a plan as an effective way of linking the house and the garden.

Waterfalls. A waterfall is best used as the source of a stream. Unless there is a natural water source, you will probably need a circulator because of the volume of water that is used. The way water falls is a result of its speed, its volume, and the arrangement of the rocks that make up the waterfall. Some of the many configurations are illustrated here. Each has a different sound quality and a different appeal in the garden, and these can be further modified by such things as a stone to split the fall in two or a flat stone at the base to project the sound.

Keep the amount of falling water constant by making a pool at the top whose overflow becomes the waterfall. Pine, maple, and chinquapin are often placed at the source of the waterfall both to disguise the water-supply system and to add charm and contrast. Mortar the stones of the waterfall in place after you have tested out your design.

Shore Protections. The edge of a pond should be at a gentle slope to create a peaceful scene. Where you intend to use the reflecting powers of the pond by placing a stone lantern or tower near its edge, keep the water level close to ground level to capture the entire image on the surface of the water. Make the shape of the pond irregular; if the pond is large, build promontories on the bank or miniature islands that appear to rise from the water. On the island put grasses and a tree or stone tower.

Some different shore protections give a Japanese touch when placed randomly along the pond's circumference. If the slope is very gentle and there is not much movement in the pond, use grass plantings—Japanese irises, eulalia, and ditch reeds—along the edge to hold the soil in place. You can also use broken or cracked stones placed in round woven baskets. Take round posts of pine that are 10 cm. in diameter and pound them in at intervals along the bank, reinforcing them with willow branches; keep their tops even. Or assemble the posts in random, zigzagging groups standing 10–30 cm. above the surface of the water. Set the wooden posts in clay; its acidity will not rot the wood as alkaline concrete will. Charring the posts before setting them prevents fungus.

If the pond is deep, use stones along the edge, either neat square blocks or larger natural stones wedged in and piled against each other. Adjust the heights of the stones visible above the water to make them look settled. Note in the illustration how bricks are used on the floor of the pond as platforms for stones that represent islets or a jagged shore.

Bridges. A bridge across a wet or dry streambed can be an attractive addition to your garden. A bridge designed merely for decoration is not unheard of, but it is safe to assume that guests, and children especially, will have an urge to test it out. All the bridge supports should be very secure. Choose materials that are appropriate to your garden. If, for example, your garden has been designed to have an "untouched" look, a simple bridge made of rough planks might be best. If you use a lot of stone themes in your garden, make a bridge out of a single granite slab. For safety, set two rocks on each side of the apron of the bridge and a lantern nearby to illuminate it at night.

Shore Protections

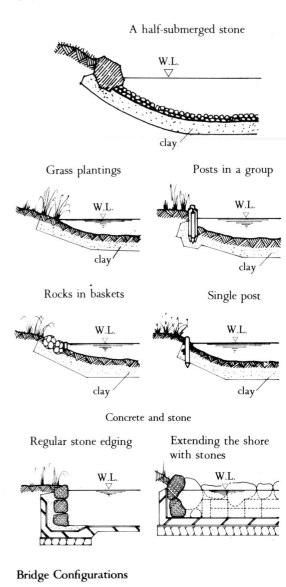

A half-submerged stone

Grass plantings

Posts in a group

Rocks in baskets

Single post

Concrete and stone

Regular stone edging

Extending the shore with stones

Bridge Configurations

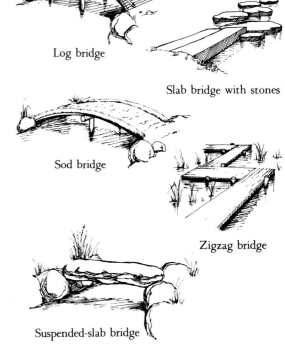

Log bridge

Slab bridge with stones

Sod bridge

Zigzag bridge

Suspended-slab bridge

BAMBOO FENCES

Fences shield, border, partition, or help unify the spaces they enclose. A designer often selects the fence first, for its height, color, and style will affect the design of the entire garden.

105. *Kinkaku-ji-gaki* (Fence of the Kinkaku-ji).

103. *Teppo-gaki* (Pipe Fence).

106. *Yarai-gaki* (Stockade Fence).

107. *Yotsume-gaki* (Four-eyed Fence).

104. *Kennin-ji-gaki* (Fence of the Kennin-ji).

108.   *Koetsu-gaki* (Koetsu Fence).

109.   *Amida-gaki* (Buddha Fence).

111.   *Katsura-gaki* (2).

110.   *Katsura-gaki* (Fence of Katsura Rikyu) (1).

112.   *Shiba-gaki* (Brushwood Fence).

113.   *Daitoku-ji-gaki* (Fence of the Daitoku-ji).

BAMBOO FENCES

The fence or wall is an essential part of the Japanese garden. Traditionally, the internal walls of the Japanese home are set with large, sliding panels; these are opened to create spacious areas indoors through which the family members can circulate freely. The home's outer walls have similar panels that, when opened, allow an unrestricted view of the garden from inside. The distant wall or fence beyond the garden is thus the only genuine barrier on the property. Echoing the architectural lines of the home and the materials of the garden, it encloses a total living area shared by house, family, and nature. It is built high enough—between 1 and 2 meters—to prevent distracting external elements from intruding.

On these two pages are very brief construction notes for the fences that appear on pages 60–61. These fences are all of typical Japanese design and vary greatly in effect and intricacy. The supporting structure of each generally consists of end posts (diam. 7.5 cm.) and inner support posts (diam. 6 cm.) of cypress, cedar, or pine, and of horizontal frame poles of bamboo (diam. 3–4 cm.). Bamboo poles (diam. 5–7 cm.) split lengthwise into semicircular pieces are often tied on as ornaments or to cover nails used in construction. Size variations are noted here where they are considered important. See pages 64–67 for other kinds of fences, gates, and walls. See pages 73–76 for more detailed notes on materials and construction. If you wish, use the examples here to help you make a Japanese-style fence of your own design.

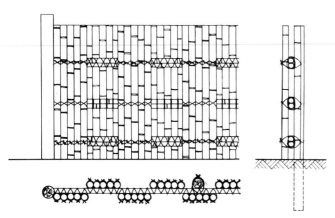

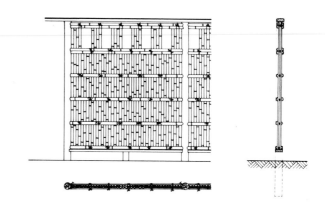

103. **Teppo-gaki.** Set up the end and inner support posts; attach the horizontal frame poles (use either one or two depending on the design). Use bamboo (diam. 6 cm.) for the vertical poles; stand them in odd-numbered groups alternately in back and front of the horizontal frame. (One variation has all the vertical poles in front of the frame.) This fence is 1–2 meters in height; use it on the property line, as a partition fence, or as a *sode-gaki* ("sleeve fence"; see also p. 66).

104. **Kennin-ji-gaki.** Set up the end and inner posts. Use split bamboo (unsplit diam. 4 cm.) for the back half of the horizontal frame. Stand split vertical poles in front of the frame and fix them temporarily at chest level. Tie on more split bamboo to make the front half of the horizontal frame. This fence is unattractive from the rear, so you can combine a front and back fence or use cedar poles or cedar bark nailed on to the back and set in place with split bamboo.

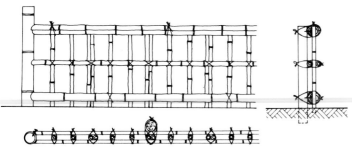

105. **Kinkaku-ji-gaki.** Set up the end and inner posts. Nail on a bamboo pole in the middle, and at the top and bottom attach lengths of split bamboo. Stand vertical bamboo poles (diam. 3 cm.) in the ground in front of the frame. In front of these vertical poles, add another horizontal round pole in the middle and split poles at top and bottom. Cover the top with another split piece whose joints have been scraped out on the inside. This fence is low and is best used in sunken areas as a substitute for a handrail.

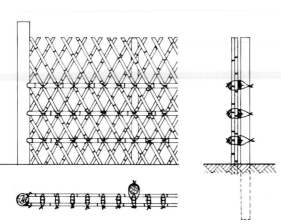

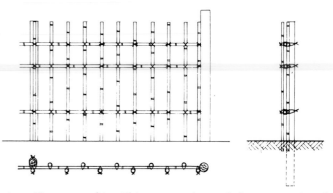

106. **Yarai-gaki.** Set up the end and inner posts. Nail on three pieces of split bamboo for the horizontal frame poles. Temporarily fix the diagonal bamboo poles to the frame poles. Tie on more horizontal split poles in front to make the frame poles look solid. The higher the fence the more toward the vertical the diagonal pieces should be to give a balanced, stable appearance.

107. **Yotsume-gaki.** This commonly used fence is made of cedar or cypress support posts and bamboo frame poles. The number of horizontal bamboo poles and the distances between them depend on the height of the fence. Usually, fences up to 1 meter have three poles, and those between 1 and 2 meters have four poles. Spacing between the horizontal poles may be regular or irregular. Complete construction procedures for this fence are given on pages 73–74.

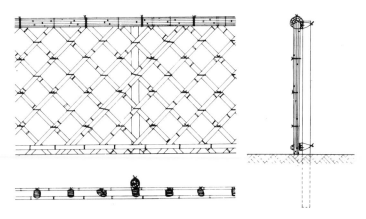

108. Koetsu-gaki. Similar in design to the *yarai-gaki*, this fence uses narrow, flat pieces of split bamboo (unsplit diam. 4 cm.) placed edge to edge to make "solid" poles, which are then attached diagonally to the frame (sometimes these poles are doubled, as shown here). Make the rail at top from narrow, split pieces (unsplit diam. 1.5 cm.) tied together in a bundle, and then cover this bundle with a wider, split piece. The fence stands 1.2–1.5 meters high and can serve as a garden partition.

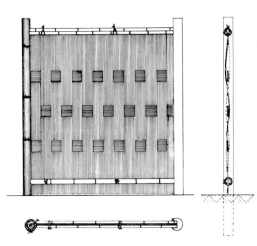

109. Amida-gaki. The horizontal and vertical pieces of bamboo that make up this fence are very thin, about 1 cm. in diameter. Set up the end posts and inner support posts. Attach split bamboo to make the horizontal frame. Make slots in the end posts into which the three horizontal groups of narrow bamboo can be inserted. After the horizontal rows are in place, weave in vertical pieces as shown. Finally, attach split bamboo to the front at top and bottom and place another split piece over the top.

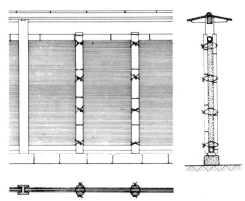

110. Katsura-gaki (1). Set up the end posts (diam. 8–10 cm.) and the inner posts. Scrape out slots in the end posts into which the frame poles and brushwood that make up the fence can be inserted. Attach the lower bamboo frame poles and vertical pieces of split bamboo in back. Pile brushwood in front, tying it tentatively to the vertical poles as you work up the fence. Then tie more vertical pieces of split bamboo in front of the fence. Finally, add the bamboo frame poles at the top.

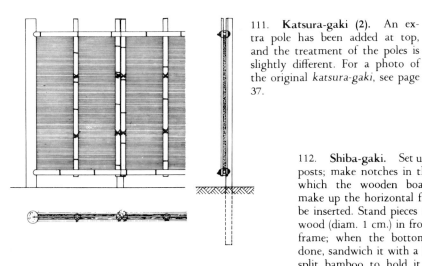

111. Katsura-gaki (2). An extra pole has been added at top, and the treatment of the poles is slightly different. For a photo of the original *katsura-gaki*, see page 37.

112. Shiba-gaki. Set up the end posts; make notches in them into which the wooden boards that make up the horizontal frame can be inserted. Stand pieces of brushwood (diam. 1 cm.) in front of the frame; when the bottom row is done, sandwich it with a length of split bamboo to hold it in place against the frame. Add more rows of brushwood on top, fixing each row in place with a split-bamboo pole as soon as it is done (this prevents the thin branches of the brushwood from shifting).

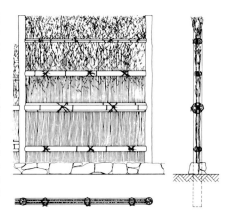

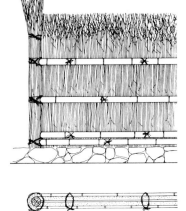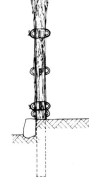

113. Daitoku-ji-gaki. This is like the *shiba-gaki*. But the end posts are wrapped in brushwood, and the fence is identical front and back.

SLEEVE FENCES, GATES, WALLS

A fence or gate in the middle of a garden can ease the transition between areas of different moods or functions. Narrow, tall fences can act as blinds to prevent intrusions into the scene observed.

115. *Gyaku chasen sode-gaki* (Upside-down Tea-Whisk Sleeve Fence).

114. *Chasen-gaki* (Tea-Whisk Fence).

116. *Koetsu sode-gaki* (Koetsu Sleeve Fence).

118. *Shiorido* (Woven-Branch Wicket).

117. *Narihira sode-gaki* (Narihira Sleeve Fence).

119. *Chumon* (Inner Gate).

120. *Dobei* (Earthen Wall).

121. *Neribei* (Mud Wall).

122. *Itabei* (Plank Wall).

123. *Ginkaku-ji-gaki* (Fence of the Ginkaku-ji).

SLEEVE FENCES, GATES, WALLS

Shorter, low, or see-through fences can be used within the garden to mark off sections with different moods (as is done in tea gardens) or to block unsightly elements from view. *Sode-gaki* ("sleeve fences") are an example of these. An apartment dweller who needs part of his balcony for storage can hide that section with a sleeve fence like the *misu-gaki* (see p. 75) to create a small alcove with room for a lantern, a stone grouping, and some potted plants. A backyard gardener can use a low fence to section off a small portion of his property to create a more manageable area in which Japanese elements can be used to full effect.

Border fences are usually fairly tall. They can be made lower, however, if there is something beyond the garden that the gardener wants to incorporate into its design—a hill, trees or shrubs, or a seacoast, for example. This technique—called *shakkei*, meaning "borrowed scenery" in Japanese—increases the garden's apparent size. And by balancing the wild with "cultivated" nature, it more vigorously unites the home and its environment. Naturally, the inner elements, which are under the gardener's control, are arranged to frame, contrast, or support the outer element that is borrowed. Some examples of this technique appear in the photo sections in the first half of this book. Unfortunately, *shakkei* can rarely be practiced in the city, which is where the effect would be most appreciated. But good opportunities sometimes present themselves. If your neighbor has a fine tree or a rustic-looking shed, don't hastily block it from view. Think of how you might use it in your design and let your fence here act not as a barrier but as a bridge.

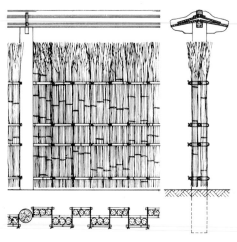

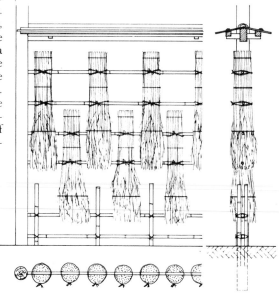

114. Chasen-gaki. Tie branches of bush clover or bamboo around a core (a long dowel will do) to make bundles 6–7 cm. in diameter. Tie each bundle with wire or string, leaving the top untied so that the branches flare out to resemble a whisk. Build the fence like the *teppo-gaki* (see p. 62), using the "whisks" in place of vertical poles. Tie short lengths of bamboo to the fronts of these bundles for decoration. The heights and widths of the "whisks" can be varied according to your design.

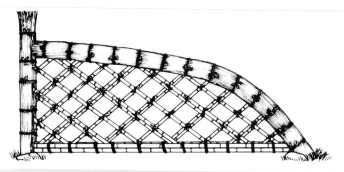

115. Gyaku chasen sode-gaki. This sleeve fence uses bundles of brushwood untied at the bottom so that they flare out to resemble a whisk. A horizontal piece of bamboo is placed through the centers of the bundles for support.

116. Koetsu sode-gaki. This low, long sleeve fence is often used to partition different areas of the garden. It resembles the *koetsu-gaki* (see p. 63) in structure and has a top rail of bundled bush clover, lindera, or split bamboo. It is rarely more than a meter high.

117. Narihira sode-gaki. This is a common example of a see-through sleeve fence. Set up thin (diam. 2 cm.) pieces of bamboo that will form the cores of the pillars that support the fence (cut out tiny wedges along the inside circumference of the bamboo so that you can bend it without its snapping where the pillar curves). Assemble thin bundles of wisteria vine, bracken, or bush clover and attach these to the bamboo pillars as you make a latticework design that stretches between the supports. Tie these bundles in place to hold the shape of the design. Finally, wrap the bamboo poles thickly in wisteria vine. If the fence is too long it will not support its weight well and will sag and look unattractive. The example shown is about 1 meter long and 1.8 meters high.

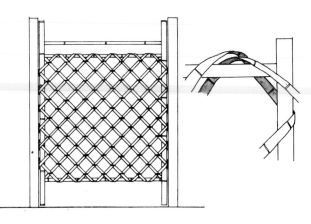

118. Shiorido. This wicket uses shaved bamboo in long strips to make the diagonal latticework; these are wrapped around the outer supports as shown. Thin, scorched branches, wisteria vine, woven bracken, or very thin bamboo can also be used in this design. Rigid materials should be tied to the frame rather than wrapped around it.

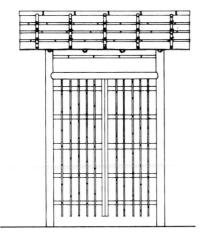

119. **Chumon.** Placed on a path to separate the inner and outer sections of a tea garden, this door can be used in your garden to separate a side yard from a front or back yard. The door is made of bamboo set on wooden slats, and the roof is of cedar bark.

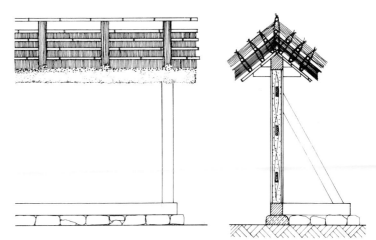

120. **Dobei.** Walls of earth or clay were in earlier times often seen around the homes and gardens of wealthy merchants. Color can be added to the clay before the wall is formed to blend with the colors in the garden. Make sure the wall is well supported in back.

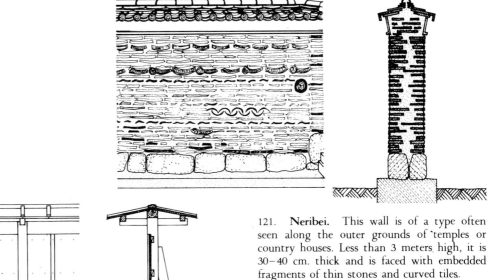

121. **Neribei.** This wall is of a type often seen along the outer grounds of temples or country houses. Less than 3 meters high, it is 30–40 cm. thick and is faced with embedded fragments of thin stones and curved tiles.

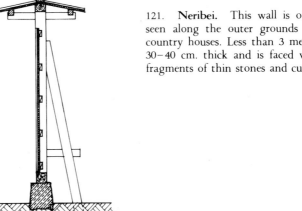

122. **Itabei.** This planked wall used to be seen around homes in middle-class urban areas. It uses painted or scorched boards of Japanese cedar, 1.2 cm. thick by 30 cm. wide.

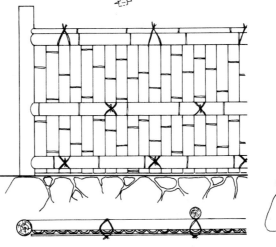

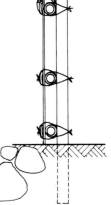

123. **Ginkaku-ji-gaki.** Different barrier elements can be combined, as shown here. The fence is in the *kennin-ji-gaki* style (see p. 62) and uses split bamboo in front and at the top.

NOTES ON BAMBOO, DWARF BAMBOO, MOSS, LOWER-STORY SHRUBS

124. Moso bamboo.

125. Castillon bamboo.

126. Kumazasa.

127. Okamezasa.

128. Haircap moss.

129. Kurama moss.

130. Aspidistra.

131. Ostrich fern.

132. Plantain lily.

Bamboo. Bamboo is a giant grass of many species. In temperate zones like Japan it thrives as a hardy, running type. The ideal site for bamboo is well-drained land gently sloping to the south. Mulch heavily to provide insulation for the root system and to keep soil temperature fairly constant.

A slightly acid heavy loam with good tilth is best. The soil is of the right consistency if it crumbles into small particles when you press a ball of it with your thumb. The deeper the soil the better, though in most cases 1 meter will suffice. Water regularly to prevent the soil from drying out. Fertilize once a year in early spring with a complete commercial fertilizer, formula 10–6–4, 50% organic, at the rate of 20–25 kg. per square meter.

Bamboo grows from 2–15 meters tall. Over time, it tends to spread its root system horizontally and to send up new culms (canes), both inside and outside the area of the original planting. To prevent congestion in the grove, cut out culms that have died, as well as some of the new shoots in spring. Periodically dig up the soil outside of the grove and hack off the laterally running rhizomes (roots) to prevent them from invading drain pipes or your neighbor's yard.

Dwarf Bamboo (*Sasa* grass). There are a number of dwarf or shrubby bamboo. Often used in the garden is *kumazasa* (*Sasa veitchii*), with leaves that turn straw-colored at the margins in autumn. It will grow in cool areas and, unlike tall bamboo, prefers the shade. Plant in a well-drained, loamy soil of good tilth, similar to the soil of a bamboo grove. Fertilize once a year, using the formula recommended for tall bamboo.

Since this plant only reaches a height of 1 meter, use it in the shade of tall garden trees, rock arrangements, or fences. In winter the leaves wither. Prune it back to the live twigs in early spring, and allow for new shoots and leaves to appear later in the spring. It withstands shearing.

Moss. Moss will not grow in dry areas but will do well where there is plenty of shade and moisture, such as the bare ground beneath spreading evergreens. It is a commonly used ground cover in the Japanese garden, for its luxuriant softness is attractive, and its water-retentive properties help preserve the land and prevent muddiness in areas where shrubs or other plantings would be too bulky. Moss will turn brown if it does not get enough water; but unless it has dried up completely it will return to green after water is added. To be on the safe side, water moss daily.

Lower-story Shrubs. Gardeners often use small groupings· of shrubs arranged about the bases of garden trees in imitation of wild shrubs and young saplings in natural landscapes. Under deciduous trees, you can use broadleaf evergreens such as aspidistra, aucuba, camellia, cotoneaster, holly, mountain laurel, mahonia, andromeda, rhododendron, or skimmia. Under needle evergreens you can place plants with, say, red berries—such as ardisia, cotoneaster, or skimmia—for color and balance. Because Japanese gardens favor the atmosphere of a forest, woody plantings should be used sparingly out in the open in areas of intense sunlight far from the shelter of trees. There are many varieties of plantings, and you will have the best results if you select from those which occur naturally in your region in sites resembling those in your garden.

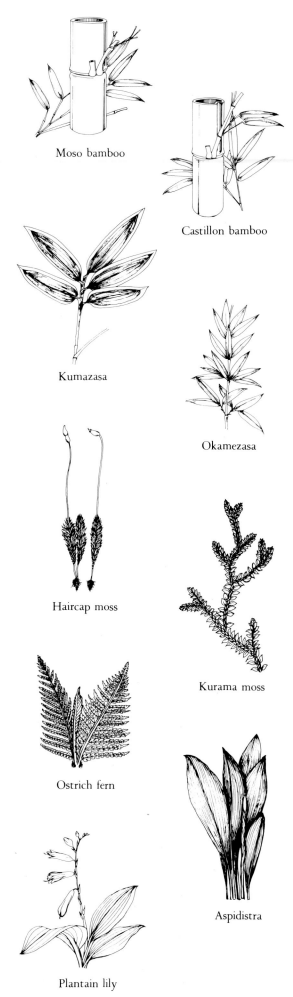

Moso bamboo

Castillon bamboo

Kumazasa

Okamezasa

Haircap moss

Kurama moss

Ostrich fern

Aspidistra

Plantain lily

1. MIDDLE-SIZE CORNER EVERGREEN:
    Longstalk holly (*Ilex pedunculosa*)
    Japanese cleyera (*Cleyera japonicum*)
    Japanese pittosporum (*Pittosporum tobira*)
2. MIDDLE-SIZE EVERGREEN TO FILL IN SPACE BETWEEN SURROUNDING TREES:
    Japanese cleyera (*Cleyera japonicum*)
    Chinese sweet osmanthus (*Osmanthus fragrans aurantiacus*)
    Japanese pittosporum (*Pittosporum tobira*)
    Japanese aralia (*Fatsia japonica*)
3. FLOWERING LOWER-STORY PLANTING FOR SHADY AREA NEAR WATERSIDE:
    Astilbe varieties
    Day lily (*Hemerocallis*)
    Balloon flower (*Platycodon grandiflorum*)
    False goat's beard (*Astilbe Buch-Ham.*)
4. LOW PLANTING TO DISGUISE TREE ROOTS:
    Dwarf satsuki azalea (*Azalea gumpo*)
    Japanese andromeda (*Pieris japonica*)
    Little-leaf box (*Buxus microphylla*)
    Coral ardisia (*Ardisia crenata [crispa]*)
    Cape jasmine (*Gardenia jasminoides*)
    Holly osmanthus (*Osmanthus ilicifolius*)
5. EVERGREEN WITH ATTRACTIVE FLOWERS:
    Camellia (*Camellia japonica*)
    Sasanqua camellia (*Camellia sasanqua*)
    Chinese sweet osmanthus (*Osmanthus fragrans aurantiacus*)
    American holly (*Ilex opaca*)
    Longstalk holly (*Ilex pedunculosa*)
6. GROUND COVER:
    Haircap moss (*Polytrichum commune*)
    Kurama moss (*Salaginella remotifolia*)
    Hikagenokazura (*Lycopodium clavatum*)
    Mondo grass (*Ophiopogon japonicus*)
    Blue rug juniper (*Juniperus horizontalis wiltoni*)
    Moss sandwort (*Arenaria verna caespitosa*)
    Bearberry (*Arctostaphylos uva-ursi*)
    Mother of thyme (*Thymus serpyllum*)
7. DECIDUOUS TREE WITH ATTRACTIVE FLOWERS, AUTUMN FOLIAGE, OR BRANCH PATTERN:
    Japanese greenleaf maple (*Acer palmatum*)
    Flowering dogwood (*Cornus florida*)
    Shadblow (*Amelanchier canadensis*)
    Amur maple (*Acer ginnala*)
    Japanese apricot (*Prunus mume*)
8. PLANTING ALONG STONE PATH:
    Kumazasa; kuma bamboo grass (*Sasa veitchii*)
    Okamezasa; okame bamboo grass (*Shibataea kumasasa*)
    Dwarf fernleaf bamboo (*Sasa disticha*)
    Palm sasa (*Sasa palmata*)
    Drooping leucothoe (*Leucothoe catesbaei*)
9. LARGE TREE AS MAIN DESIGN ELEMENT:
    Japanese black pine (*Pinus thunbergii*)
    Japanese red pine (*Pinus densiflora*)
    Tanyosho pine (*Pinus densiflora umbraculifera*)
    Japanese cedar (*Cryptomeria japonica*)
    Japanese cypress (*Chamaecyparis obtusa*)
    Carolina hemlock (*Tsuga caroliniana*)
    Canadian hemlock (*Tsuga canadensis*)
10. EVERGREEN THAT DOESN'T BLOCK LARGE TREE BEHIND:
    Mountain laurel (*Kalmia latifolia*)
    Red photinia (*Photinia frazieri*)
    Laurel; sweet bay (*Laurus nobilis*)
    Chinese sweet osmanthus (*Osmanthus fragrans aurantiacus*)
11. SHRUB WITH ATTRACTIVE FLOWERS:
    Japanese quince (*Chaenomeles lagenaria*)
    Redvein enkianthus (*Enkianthus campanulatus*)
    Lilac (*Syringa vulgaris*)
    Pink weigela (*Weigela rosea*)
    Japanese house hydrangea (*Hydrangea macrophylla*)

These two pages show a typical, if somewhat idealized, layout of the plantings in a good-sized Japanese garden. The gardener selected the points for placing the main stones and trees by using the point-plotting system explained on page 39. Because north gets the most sun, it has been used as the main planting area.

The trees in the northeast corner represent a forest. A lantern is placed in their midst. The *tsukubai* and *shishi odoshi* are on the edge of the "forest," with sand and pebbles scattered about for drainage. The sand and pebbles spread out to create a "sea." Stones form a dry landscape, and there is a bamboo forest behind to develop the southeast corner. Throughout, moss, ferns, shrubs, and grasses fill in the garden's lower story. Small trees and shrubs that flower at different times of the year are scattered about to counterpoint the larger evergreens with color and seasonal change. Low, undulating, mounded hedges are planted near the dry

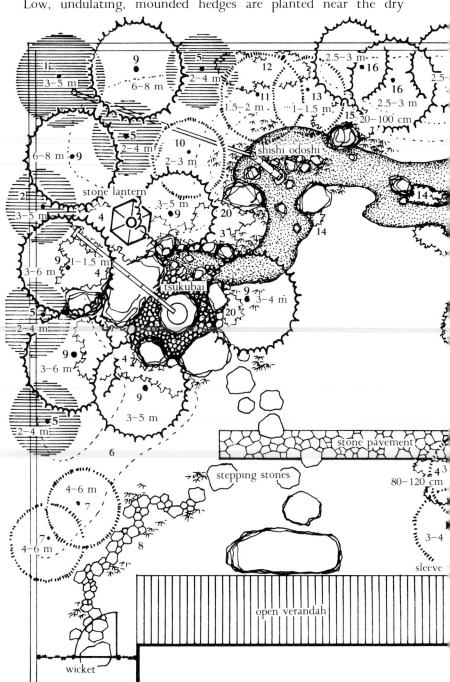

landscape to give greater depth and a stronger permanent structure to the garden's design.

The names of various trees, shrubs, and ground covers are given outside the layout as examples of possible planting patterns and themes. These are keyed by number to the sites in the garden. The recommended planting for each site is listed first (common name followed by scientific name); following are substitute varieties. All the plants listed here can be obtained and grown in North America. Check with your local nursery to find out which are appropriate to the climate or soil of your region. For more varieties, consult the reference books listed on pages 77–78.

In these lists, a tree is sometimes listed under a shrub heading and vice versa. This means that the tree or shrub is shaped and pruned into that new role. The heights of all plantings should be controlled to keep the garden elements in balance; because many of the plants in the garden, if not cut back, will grow higher than is appropriate to their sites, yearly attention is a must. But you should anticipate growth and select your plantings based on how you envision the garden after several years have passed.

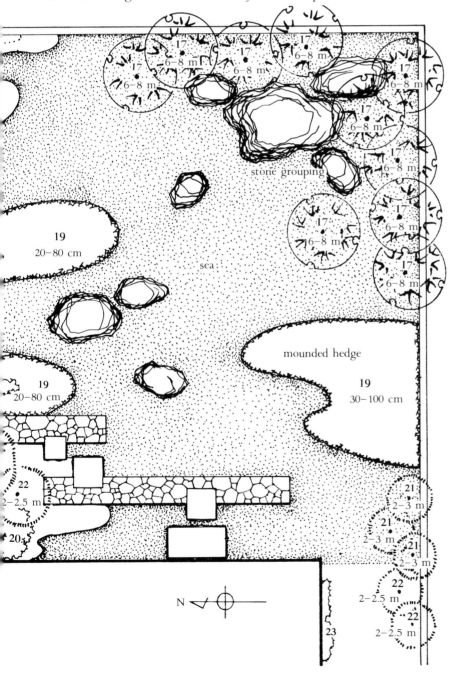

12. LOWER-STORY PLANTING FOR SHADY AREA:
Funkia; plantain lily (*Hosta fortunei*)
European solomon seal (*Polygonatum japonicum*)
Aspidistra (*Aspidistra elatior*)

13. SHRUB WITH ATTRACTIVE FLOWERS OR FRUIT:
Doublefile viburnum (*Viburnum tomentosum*)
Weeping forsythia (*Forsythia suspensa*)
White enkianthus (*Enkianthus perulatus*)
Pink weigela (*Weigela rosea*)
Japanese house hydrangea (*Hydrangea macrophylla*)

14. LOW PLANTING TO SET AROUND A LARGE STONE:
Christmas fern (*Polystichum acrostichoides*)
Ostrich fern (*Matteuccia struthiopteris*)
Lily turf (*Liriope muscari spicata*)
Drooping leucothoe (*Leucothoe catesbaei*)

15. PLANTING TO DISGUISE TREE ROOTS:
Coral ardisia (*Ardisia crenata* [*crispa*])
Indian azalea (*Rhododendron indicum*)
Japanese nandina (*Nandina domestica*)
Japanese andromeda (*Pieris japonica*)
Cape jasmine (*Gardenia jasminoides*)
Plantain lily (*Hosta undulata*)

16. TREE WITH ATTRACTIVE FLOWERS, FRUIT, OR BRANCH PATTERN:
Japanese greenleaf maple (*Acer palmatum*)
Winged spindle tree (*Euonymus alatus*)
Amur maple (*Acer ginnala*)
Flowering dogwood (*Cornus florida*)
Yoshino cherry (*Prunus yedoensis*)

17. BAMBOO TO ACCENT STONE GROUPING:
Yellow-groove bamboo (*Phyllostachys aureo-sulcata*)
Chekiang hardy bamboo (*Phyllostachys nuda*)
Matake; Castillon bamboo (*Phyllostachys bambusoides*)
Hachiku; Henon bamboo (*Phyllostachys nigra henonis*)
Kurochiku; black bamboo (*Phyllostachys nigra*)
Narihira bamboo (*Semiarundinaria fastuosa*)

18. FLOWERING TREE OR SHRUB:
Japanese apricot (*Prunus mume*)
Apricot (*Prunus armeniaca*)
Chinese Judas tree (*Cercis chinensis*)
Yoshino cherry (*Prunus yedoensis*)
Japanese quince (*Chaenomeles lagenaria*)

19. LOW, MOUNDED HEDGE:
Dwarf satsuki azalea (*Azalea gumpo*)
Hybrid evergreen azalea (*Azalea kurume*)
Korean box (*Buxus microphylla koreana*)
Dwarf Japanese holly (*Ilex crenata helleri*)
Fortune's osmanthus (*Osmanthus fortunei*)
Holly osmanthus (*Osmanthus ilicifolius*)

20. LOWER-STORY PLANTING IN A SMALL GROUPING:
Plantain lily (*Hosta undulata*)
Japanese nandina (*Nandina domestica*)
Eulalia (*Miscanthus sinensis*)
Scouring rush; horsetail (*Equisetum hiemale japonicum*)

21. FLOWERING SHRUB:
Redvein enkianthus (*Enkianthus campanulatus*)
White enkianthus (*Enkianthus perulatus*)
Weeping forsythia (*Forsythia suspensa*)
Kerria (*Kerria japonica*)

22. FLOWERING SHRUB:
Bridalworth spirea (*Spiraea prunifolia plena*)
Anthony Waterer spirea (*Spiraea bumalda* 'A. Waterer')
Redvein enkianthus (*Enkianthus campanulatus*)
Japanese quince (*Chaenomeles lagenaria*)
Lilac (*Syringa vulgaris*)

23. LOWER-STORY PLANTING:
Plantain lily (*Hosta undulata*)
Iris (*Iris japonica*)
Scouring rush; horsetail (*Equisetum hiemale japonicum*)

TREES: SHAPING AND PRUNING

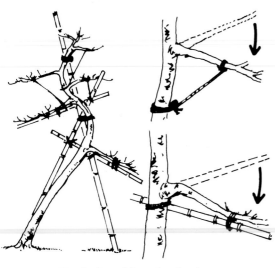

Remove branches alternately right and left

Give the trunk an S-curve

Fix the lateral branches in place

Trim the needle clusters and prune off excess branches to give the tree balance and clean lines

Shaping. The Japanese gardener shapes his trees to expose their true qualities and to give them a balanced form that harmonizes with the rest of the garden. Most tree configurations are derived from actual examples seen in areas that are well-exposed to the elements, such as a seashore or a mountaintop; in effect they make the garden trees look old before their time. The amount of control involved here gets to the very heart of Japanese gardening, for it is these "artificial," human methods—like shaping—that develop the garden's primeval naturalism and air of permanence.

A common method used for shaping a black pine, a yew, or a Japanese holly is presented here. The trunk of the tree is given an S-curve, and the needles along the branches are shaped into globular clusters that balance each other left and right and top to bottom. Begin in May or June with a young, pliant sapling (about 2 meters high) either taken from the countryside or grown in a nursery. Plant it diagonally in the ground. Cut off branches alternately right and left along the main trunk (the dotted lines in the illustration) so that they won't interfere with other branches as the tree grows. Bend the trunk as shown and hold the bends in place with fixed poles.

Fix the forms of the horizontal branches with rope or with lateral poles as shown (be careful that the rope doesn't dig into the bark; use a rubber plate between the rope and the branch it is tied to). Pull the branches a little to the front and back of the tree so that the tree will fill up about the trunk and not look symmetrical. Now prune the small branches that lie along the bottoms of the main branches to develop the shapes of the needle clusters. Keep the poles in place until the tree will hold its new shape without them—about one to two years.

Pruning. Pruning is not just for shaping. It ventilates the tree, permits sunlight to reach it all over, prevents disease and pest infestation, develops strength and durability, and improves the quality of its fruits and flowers. Pruning may be done at any time of the year, but it is usually done in spring after the sap ceases to flow, or after blooming in the case of a flowering tree or shrub. Prune branches that detract from or confuse the desired effect, dead branches, sick branches, branches growing between the shaped branches, and branches thrust up from the roots. Suckers that grow vertically, run parallel, or cross should also be removed to neaten the lines. The thick lateral branches on the concave bends of the S-curved main trunk should be cut so that they are shorter than those on the convex bends This balances the overall design. Apply tree-wound paint to any scar larger than 5–6 mm. in diameter. Use a dark paint that will blend the light-colored scar into the surrounding wood.

MAKING FENCES

Two fences that are easy to make and commonly used in the Japanese garden are presented here. The *yotsume-gaki* ("four-eyed fence") is a bamboo lattice-fence of medium height; it can stand on its own or be placed behind a row of tall trees on the border of the property. The *misu-gaki* ("bamboo-blind fence") is a *sode-gaki* ("sleeve fence") placed along a building to act as a windbreak or to hide unattractive or contrasting elements from the view of the garden; it is in the style of a bamboo screen. The special knot used for these fences is explained on page 76. Climate and upkeep are important factors that affect the lifespan of a bamboo fence, but under good conditions it can be expected to last ten years before replacement becomes necessary.

Tools for making fences

Small shovel or trowel for digging holes
Hammer for driving nails
Flat stone or soft mallet for pounding bamboo
Medium-tooth saw for cutting wood
Fine-tooth saw for cutting bamboo
Knife for splitting bamboo
Augur or drill for making holes in bamboo
Measuring rule or tape
Plumb rule
Brush for applying wood preservative
Straw brush for cleaning
String for aligning poles ("guide string")

Yotsume-gaki

The *yotsume-gaki* is a bamboo lattice fence of medium height. Its supporting structure consists of two wooden end posts, higher than the fence proper, and wooden inner support posts at the level of the fence and spaced 180 cm. apart. The frame is made of horizontal and vertical lengths of bamboo. The vertical pieces stand alternately in front and back of the horizontal ones. The fence can be of any length; the builder extends it by inserting narrow tips of bamboo into wider, open bases.

SELECTING MATERIALS: *Wooden posts*. The end posts and inner support posts may be of an inexpensive wood like pine, but cedar will probably look better and last longer. The posts should be straight with no splits or knots; the bark should be stripped and the surface clean. End posts are 140 cm. long and 7.5 cm. in diameter; inner support posts are 130 cm. long and 6 cm. in diameter.
Bamboo. Cut the horizontal and vertical frame poles from pieces of bamboo that are about 5 meters long and 3–4 cm. in diameter (see the note in **5**). You will need about 15 lengths of bamboo for every 6–7 meters of fencing. Unless you are very fortunate, not every part of the bamboo will be usable because of warps, bruises, or bad placement of joints. The best bamboo comes from temperate areas (it deteriorates slowly); bamboo cut in winter is more durable than that cut in summer. Green, fresh-cut bamboo is recommended in Japan, but in North America and Europe such good material is rarely available. If you can't find bamboo at all, white cedar can be used instead; the effect, of course, is not the same.
Twine. Twine is used to tie the vertical and horizontal frame poles together. Choose a rot-proof, well-twisted variety that is dyed black to contrast with the color of the bamboo. It is used doubled up, and you will need about 27 meters for every 2 meters of fencing.
Nails. Use zinc nails 6–7.5 cm. long.

PREPARATION: Clear the ground of rocks, plants, and bumps. Apply wood preservative to the parts of the end posts and inner support posts that are to be buried in the ground. You may char the posts to get the same effect; clean the parts that will remain above the ground with a straw brush and water.

Yotsume-gaki

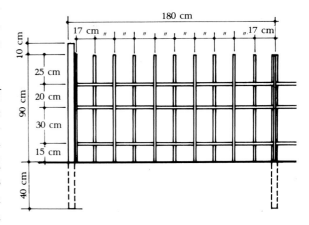

Dimensions

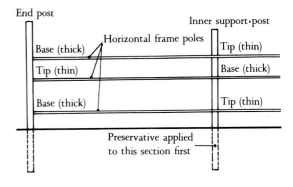

Arrangement of posts and horizontal bamboo

73

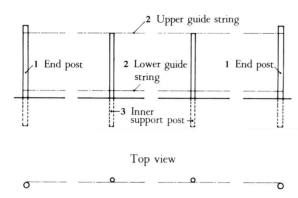

Top view

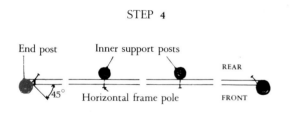

The lower guide string marks the rear surfaces of the end posts and the front surfaces of the inner support posts

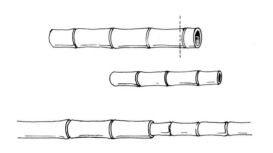

Extend a frame pole by inserting a narrow tip into a base

STEP 4

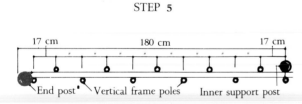

STEP 5

CONSTRUCTION: **1** *End posts.* At each end of the fence, dig a hole about 40 cm. deep. Insert the end post and, after making sure it is straight, pack in soil around it to fill up the hole.

2 *Guide strings.* Run a guide string between the two end posts; attach it at a point 10 cm. below their tops to mark the height of the frame. To prevent the guide string from sagging, tack it to the tops of the inner support posts after they are in place (step **3**).

Run another guide string between the rear surfaces of the end posts to determine the placement of the inner support posts.

3 *Inner support posts.* The inner support posts are 180 cm. apart; align their tops with the upper guide string and use the lower guide string to line up their front surfaces with the rear surfaces of the end posts. Sink the posts 40 cm. into the ground. Remove the lower guide string.

On each post mark the points where the horizontal parts of the frame (in **4**) will be nailed on; each horizontal pole and its extension should be parallel to the ground the length of the fence.

4 *Horizontal frame poles.* Take straight pieces of bamboo and clean each one with a straw brush. Each pole has a base (thick end, near the root) and a tip (narrow end). The frame begins at an end post with the ends of the horizontal lengths of bamboo alternately base and tip from the top down. To attach the bamboo to the end post, saw it just below (or above) a joint at a 45° angle and drill a hole in the uncut section near the joint. Place this section flush along the rear surface of the end post and attach it there by driving a nail through the hole. Be careful not to strike the bamboo with the hammer or punch the head of the nail into its delicate fiber.

Extend a pole by inserting a narrow tip into a wider base.

Drill holes into the horizontal poles and nail them onto the inner support posts as you reach them. Finally, at the second end post, cut each bamboo pole at a 45° angle, drill a hole, and nail it on.

Apply preservative to the untreated parts of the wooden posts.

5 *Vertical frame poles.* Vertical frame poles should be spaced 17 cm. apart the length of the fence, with one on the inside edge of each end post and one directly in front of each inner support post.

Cut the vertical frame poles from the thicker ends of the bamboo toward the base. The length of each piece should be a bit more than the height of the fence, and what will be the top should end in a joint to prevent water from collecting inside the bamboo. Place the poles alternately in front and back of the horizontal frame poles. Pound on them gently with a mallet or soft stone until they stand on their own and their tops are aligned with the guide string. Taper a base if necessary to drive it into the ground. If a base won't go in at all, cut the pole and fix it temporarily to the horizontal frame with string or tape.

6 *Tying the frame.* Using twine, tie the frame to the inner support posts from the rear. Then tie the junctions of the vertical and horizontal frame poles, checking all the time to make sure that everything is properly positioned. The vertical poles alternate front and back; tie each pole from the side of the frame it stands on and from the bottom to the top. After tying the frame, check verticals, horizontals, and heights. Remove the guide string.

Misu-gaki

The *misu-gaki* is a sleeve fence designed to look like a bamboo screen. It can be used to block out unwanted elements from view or to extend the corner of the house into the garden. Horizontal rows of bamboo are nailed onto two vertical wooden posts. Split, semicircular bamboo lengths are then tied to the vertical posts to hide the nails.

SELECTING MATERIALS: For the vertical posts use two pieces of pine or cedar, each 240 cm. long and 6 cm. in diameter. Use green bamboo, as explained on page 73, for the horizontal rows; you will need approximately 55 pieces 150 cm. long and 3 cm. in diameter. Half should be cut just below a joint toward the base of the bamboo, and half should be cut just above a joint toward the tip. Two vertical lengths of bamboo that will be split to cover the nails should each be 2 meters long and 3–4 cm. in diameter. You will need 110 zinc nails, 4.5 cm. long.

PREPARATION: Char the wooden posts. Rub them with a straw brush, clean them with water, and put them aside to dry.

Make a marking guide for drilling holes in the horizontal pieces of bamboo out of a length of lumber attached to a platform; the platform represents the wall of the house and two marks on the lumber, 110 cm. apart, show where the bamboo is to be nailed to the vertical posts. Place the "jointless" end of each piece of bamboo against the platform before drilling above the marks on the lumber. Make sure the length of bamboo is perfectly straight or that a bow in the bamboo will not be visible when the fence is viewed from the front.

Pound a knife along a longitudinal section of each vertical piece of bamboo and split it into two semicircular pieces.

CONSTRUCTION: 1   *Vertical posts.* Set the first vertical post 20 cm. from the edge of the house. Set the second pole 110 cm. away from the first; the line from the two poles to the house is perpendicular. Sink the posts about 50 cm. into the ground, leaving 190 cm. above.

2   *Horizontal bamboo.* Attach a plumb rule to the tops of the vertical posts and let the plumb line hang down 150 cm. from the edge of the house.

Starting 10 cm. from the top of the vertical support posts, nail on lengths of bamboo parallel to the ground. Set each directly below the one above it. Alternate pieces cut with the joint at tip and base, always placing the joint on the side of the fence away from the wall and flush with the plumb line. Continue adding bamboo down the vertical posts to a point 15 cm. above the ground.

3   *Split, vertical bamboo.* Use the split pieces of bamboo to cover the nails that are lined up along the vertical posts. Pound these pieces down from the top until they stand on their own in the ground. Then tie each one to its post with five knots, each knot encompassing two of the horizontal pieces. Finally, tie the two remaining split pieces to the backs of the vertical posts.

STEP 1

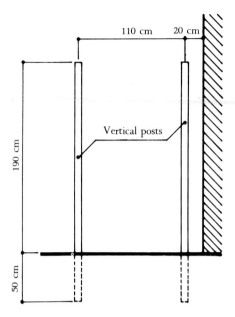

STEP 2

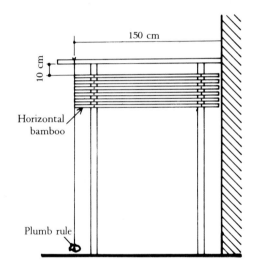

STEP 3

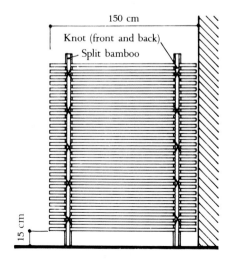

TYING THE KNOT FOR THE YOTSUME-GAKI

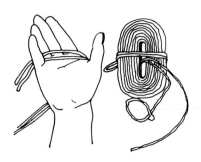 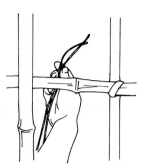 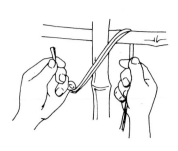 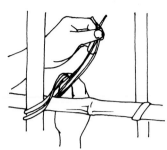

1, 2. Double-strand the twine by rewrapping it. Wet the new bundle; wet twine is easier to use and will pull tight on the frame as it dries.

3. With your right hand, pass the twine under the horizontal pole (bottom right of the intersection) all the way to the back of the frame.

4. Take the end in your left hand. Pull it toward you, over the horizontal pole (top right), to the front of the frame.

5. Wrap the twine around the vertical pole (bottom left) and, letting go of it briefly, pass it under the long end in back.

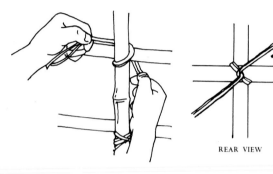 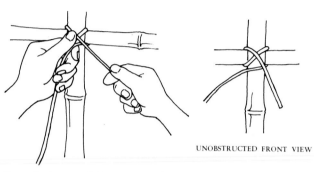

REAR VIEW

UNOBSTRUCTED FRONT VIEW

6. Push with both arms crossed until the twine is snug where it crosses behind the frame. Then pull the short end to the front of the frame (top left).

7. Cross the long and short ends in front of the vertical pole. The short end should be on top; hold it with your right hand and pull on it for tension. Fix the intersection in front by pinching it with your left thumb and forefinger. Hold your left hand in this position through step **11.**

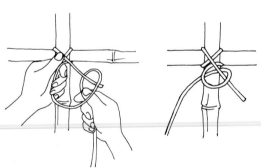 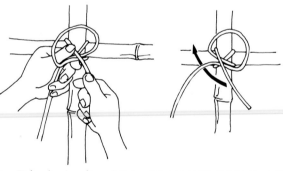

8. Let go of the short end. With your right hand, take up the dangling long end and use it to make a loop that passes clockwise over and around the short end. Fix the part of the long end that completes the loop between your left thumb and forefinger to hold the loop in place.

9. Take the dangling short end in your right hand. Push it up to the left and, after you pass it under your left arm, pinch its base with the fingers of your left hand.

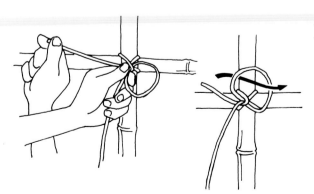 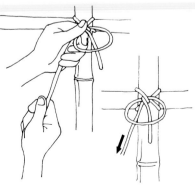 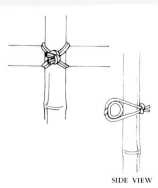

SIDE VIEW

10. Push the short end through the loop. Once it is through, pull it snug until it is caught again in the pinch of your left hand.

11. Let go of the short end. Pull the long end with your right hand until the knot is secure.

12. Clip the ends to about 2 cm. Now practice the knot until the hand motions become automatic.

FOR FURTHER REFERENCE

Books You Can Use

ON JAPANESE GARDENS

Asano, Kiichi, and Takakura, Gisei. *Japanese Gardens Revisited.* Rutland, Vt. and Tokyo: Charles E. Tuttle, 1973.

Mainly a picture book but has very high quality photos.

Engel, David H. *Japanese Gardens for Today.* Rutland, Vt. and Tokyo: Charles E. Tuttle, 1959.

A practical explanation of the basic rules. Well illustrated with photos in black and white and in color.

Ito, Teiji, and Iwamiya, Takeji. *The Japanese Garden: An Approach to Nature.* New Haven: Yale University Press, 1972.

Historical and interpretive on the spirit and philosophy of Japanese gardens. Beautifully illustrated with photos in black and white and in color.

Kitamura, Fumio, and Ishizu, Yurio. *Garden Plants in Japan.* Tokyo: Kokusai Bunka Shinkokai (Society for International Cultural Relations), 1963.

A thoroughly annotated plant list, cross-indexed by Japanese common names, American common names, and botanical names. Contains useful information on habitats, character, descriptions, culture, soil, foliage, flowers, and so on. Illustrated. An important part of any library on Japanese gardens.

Kuck, Loraine. *The World of the Japanese Garden: From Chinese Origins to Modern Landscape Art.* New York and Tokyo: Walker/Weatherhill, 1968.

An expanded and revised edition of the author's earlier *The Art of Japanese Gardens* (New York: John Day Co., 1940). Like that work, a well-researched and complete historical and interpretive study.

Saito, Katsuo. *Japanese Gardening Hints.* Tokyo: Japan Publications, 1969.

Contains many helpful explanations on design, construction, and the reasons why. Illustrated with photos and line drawings.

————, and Wada, Sadaji. *Magic of Trees and Stones: Secrets of Japanese Gardening.* New York and Tokyo: JPT Book Co., 1964.

Contains graphic explanations and is well illustrated on construction. Also has some information on construction of ponds and waterfalls.

ON GENERAL LANDSCAPE DESIGN, CONSTRUCTION, PLANT MATERIALS

Hubbard, Henry V., and Kimball, Theodora. *An Introduction to the Study of Landscape Design.* New York: Macmillan, 1924.

The acknowledged classic. Though old, what it says is still valid.

Perry, Frances. *The Garden Pool.* New York and South Brunswick, N.J.: Great Albion Books, 1972.

Though directed mainly to builders of water features in Western gardens, it contains many valuable hints with universal application.

Sunset Books. *Garden Pools, Fountains and Waterfalls.* Menlo Park, Calif.: Lane Books, 1974.

Has a good chapter on naturalistic streams, falls, and ponds.

Swindells, Philip. *A Guide to Water Gardening.* New York: Charles Scribner's Sons, 1975.

Contains helpful information for pool builders.

Warring, Ron. *Garden Pools and Fishponds.* London: Stanley Paul, 1971.

Has six chapters of useful information on construction.

Wyman, Donald. *Ground Cover Plants.* New York: Macmillan, 1950.

————. *Shrubs and Vines for American Gardens.* New York: Macmillan, 1953.

————. *Trees for American Gardens.* New York: Macmillan, 1956.

All three books by Wyman are a must for any American or Canadian gardener. Extremely useful and complete.

Japanese Gardens You Can Visit

Brooklyn Botanic Garden, Brooklyn, N.Y.
Extensive Japanese stroll garden with pond and a replica of the Ryoan-ji garden.

Duke Gardens, Somerville, N.J. Tel.: (201) 722–3700.
Acres of gardens under glass, including a Japanese garden. Call first for hours and reservations.

Golden Gate Park, San Francisco, Calif.
An extensive Japanese garden dating from an international exposition many decades ago.

Gulf States Paper Corporation, P.O. Box 3199, Tuscaloosa, Ala. Tel.: (205) 553–6200.
A corporate headquarters, consisting of four Heian-period-style pavilions set around a Japanese garden. Call for appointment.

Hillwood Museum Gardens, 4155 Linnean Avenue, N.W., Washington, D.C.
A Japanese garden within the extensive estate of the late Marjorie Merriweather Post. May be visited, but reserve two weeks in advance. Send $2.00 with reservation. Open Monday, Wednesday, Friday, and Saturday, 9:30–11:30 and 1:30–3:30.

The Morikami, Yamato Colony, Palm Beach County, Fla.
Gardens and a museum. Write the director for admission details.

Oriental Stroll Garden, Hammond Museum, North Salem, N.Y.
Write the director for admission details.

Seiwa-en, Missouri Botanical Garden, St. Louis, Mo.
A large Japanese garden, recently completed.

Tennessee Botanical Gardens and Fine Arts Center, Cheekwood, Nashville, Tenn.
A Japanese hill garden and stroll garden with viewing pavilion. Under construction; expect completion 1980–81.

Places You Can Buy Materials

USA

Rafu Shoten, 309 East First Street, Los Angeles, Ca. 90012.

Soko Hardware Co., 1698 Post Street, San Francisco, Ca. 94115.

Komoto Department Store, 1528 Kern Street, Fresno, Ca. 93706.

Kogura Co., 231 East Jackson Street, San Jose, Ca. 95112.

Uwajimaya, 519 Sixth Avenue South, Seattle, Wash. 98104.

Toguri Mercantile Co., 851–53 West Belmont Avenue, Chicago, Ill. 60657.

Oriental Imports, 1118 South Orange Avenue, Orlando, Fla. 32801.

Katagiri and Co., Inc., 224 East Fifty-ninth Street, New York, N.Y. 10022.

Toyo Trading Co., 225 Fifth Avenue, New York, N.Y. 10016.

The above companies sell stone lanterns, water basins, towers, and sculpture from Japan and other countries of the Orient.

Bamboo & Rattan Works, 901 Jefferson St., Hoboken, N.J. or The Otto Gerdau Company, 82 Wall St., New York, N.Y.

Both companies sell seasoned bamboo from Japan and Taiwan. The bamboo is chemically treated to retard mold and is available in all lengths. Diameters range from pencil-thin to 12.5 cm.

H. E. Fletcher Co., West Chelmsford, Mass. or Gran-i-grit, Mt. Airy, N.C.

Both companies sell fowl grits made of crushed granite. Order 2 parts turkey (medium) to 3 parts hen (fine) to get a good mix you can use in a sand garden.

JAPAN

Wado Industry Co., Ltd., Koide Building, Ikutamamae-cho 90, Tennoji-ku, Osaka, Japan. Telex: WADOOL J64844.

Sells roof tiles for walls, fences, buildings.

Mr. Yasaburo Fujiwara, Daitoku-ji-mae, Murasakino-Monzencho, Kita-ku, Kyoto 603, Japan.

Sells stone garden artifacts, antique and new.

About Measurements

The measurements in this book are all given in metric units, as they are in Japan. These are mostly rounded figures that suggest approximate dimensions, and the reader need not follow them strictly. Measurements in the sections on fences are given more precisely, but even here the reader will find that he has considerable leeway in applying them. Readers unfamiliar with metric units can use the following chart to get rough equivalents in feet and inches.

To go from:	Multiply:
Millimeters (mm.) → inches	# of mm. by 0.04
Centimeters (cm.) → inches	# of cm. by 0.4
Meters (m.) → feet	# of m. by 3.3

INDEX TO TEXT AND PHOTOS

References to text pages are in roman type. Selected photos that offer good examples of how particular elements are used in the garden are indicated by their numbers in bold type.